IN SEARCH OF THE HI

A startling and exciting investigation (
has baffled and fascinated m:

In Search
of the
Healing
Energy

MARY CODDINGTON
Foreword by William Gutman M.D.

DESTINY BOOKS
New York

Destiny Books
377 Park Avenue South
New York, NY 10016

First quality paperback edition: October 1983

10 9 8 7 6 5 4 3 2

Library of Congress Cataloging in Publication Data

Coddington, Mary.
  In search of the healing energy.

  Bibliography: p.
  Includes index.
  1. Therapeutic systems.   2. Therapeutics, Suggestive.
3. Mind and body.   I. Title.
R733.C62   1983   615.5′3   83-18952
ISBN 0-89281-051-3

Destiny Books is a division of Inner Traditions International, Ltd.

Printed and bound in the United States of America.

ACKNOWLEDGEMENTS

In addition to the many individuals and sources referred to in the text, I am also indebted to the following for their advice and support: Adele Behar, Yolanda Betegh, Henrietta Cholmeley-Jones, Frank Don, Susanne Frew, Thelma Gordon, Gordon Hendricks, Murray Herman, Joseph Holohan, Loris Hoyt, Larry Katz, Elliott Lampert, Sara Moadel, Charles Normandin, Boris Ostrovsky, Fred Paddock, Ann Pastorelli, Rev. Melvin Smith, Charles Tekeyan, Bertha Youhas, and Thomas Zimmer.

For Lyman, Jane, and Peter

CONTENTS

FOREWORD

One of the greatest adventures of all time has been the age-old quest for a mysterious healing energy – an energy with the ability to make apparent 'miracles' and to transform not only medicine but life itself.

This very timely and immensely engrossing book traces man's strange encounters with this force and describes the many therapeutic methods that appear to rely on it, either directly or indirectly.

One might conceive of this inscrutable phenomenon as the *vis formativa*, the formative energy or creative force that shapes everything in its own specific 'gestalt' or form: crystal, plant, animal, and man himself can never be explained causally – because the reason why material atoms assemble in one form rather than another is due precisely to this *vis formativa*, a superior energy that uses the causal connection in the same way that an architect's idea makes use of bricks and mortar to create a livable structure.

The *vis formativa* might also be perceived as the spiritual blueprint of material forms ...

It is the force that causes the lost tail of a lizard to regenerate in its specific form.

It is the force that causes the renewal of our damaged skin cells, always directing the creation of exact replicas of those that were lost.

It is the force that pervades each organ in order to produce regeneration or healing.

The greatest physicists of our time, Einstein and Planck, recognized an energy beyond the material – a creative power that brings about the marvellous order of the universe and of each being and object in the universe. In this ordering, forming energy that pervades everything lies the basis of the healing force.

The following pages are sure to heighten interest in this oldest of all mysteries.

William Gutman, M.D.

PREFACE

The search for a specific unknown energy, an energy with the power to heal, has obsessed the human mind and spirit since the beginning of civilization. For centuries, men of genius have tried to harness this strange, enigmatic force and enlist it to the aid of science. Thus far, however, it has remained slightly out of grasp, eluding its would-be captors with an almost capricious tenacity and always escaping definition. Casting a spell that could curse or bless those who fell beneath it, this phenomenon and its pursuit cost many scientists and physicians their reputations; yet they gloried in the chase.

Throughout these pages, the energy is traced from a period of prehistory to modern times with a description of its various advocates: the ancient kahunas, Pythagoras, Hippocrates, Paracelsus, Mesmer, von Reichenbach, Hahnemann, Palmer, Reich, and others. Although it is revealed in a different way to each and receives a different name from each, the healing energy always displays a remarkable similarity.

In the process of researching this book and compiling the many excerpts that are included, I became increasingly aware that the healing energy involved far more than healing. Frequently related to certain powers of the mind and portrayed as having an intelligence of its own, the phenomenon began to emerge as a part of consciousness itself.

There is little known, generally, about consciousness or even the processes of human thought. But the findings of modern physics — the convertibility of matter and energy, the wave-particle duality, the subatomic particles, anti-particles, and especially the role of the scientist's own observation — have shattered the old mechanistic, computerlike view of man's awareness.

As a result, exploring the true nature of consciousness has become a major occupation. It is , some feel, at the very cutting edge of current thought – thought that is giving birth to a new ontology or science of being that recognizes man as a holistic unit of body-mind-spirit, whose primary purpose in life is to participate in the evolution of consciousness, both individual and collective. The healing energy, as we shall see, is an essential ingredient in this area.

The following pages, then, begin with medicine and extend to the broader realms of consciousness. By presenting the writings and opinions of those scientists and doctors who have so diligently pursued it, I hope that the healing energy will appear as a valid theoretical concept, one that may provide the links not only between the medicine of today and the healing of tomorrow but also between physics and metaphysics, the normal and paranormal.

Still unharnessed, this mysterious force continues to haunt the imaginations of contemporary seekers who believe in its great promise for humanity. Perhaps you, too, will join the search ...

1

INTRODUCTION:
WHY THE SEARCH?

There can no longer be any doubt that we are living in the midst of a revolution, a revolution that exists, fortunately, in the bloodless realm of thought. To some, this new surge of heightened awareness is known as the age of Aquarius; to others, it is the psychic era. Many believe it to be the natural evolution of ideas; and more than a few think we are simply rediscovering old ones. Of one thing we may be sure: a new consciousness has been born, and it permeates every aspect of our culture, from lifestyle to medicine.

Never before has the pursuit of health absorbed so many people so much of the time. As a result, modern medicine has been subject to a growing public scrutiny. Such scrutiny includes much praise for the giant strides made in the control of many illnesses and certainly in surgical techniques; it also includes the observation that most doctors, perhaps because so many epidemic diseases have been conquered, tend to concentrate on pathology rather than prevention. Symptoms are treated after disease has set in, and the drugs used to alleviate these symptoms sometimes cause more harm than good. In fact, a whole new set of illnesses, known as iatrogenic (doctor-induced) diseases, has been created from the use of certain drugs.

Energy and Matter

What one hopes is that medical science, without neglecting the areas of its present focus, will also seek a unifying and preventive factor in the realm of healing. Medical research, for example, might probe more deeply into the possibility of relating certain new findings in physics to the human body, or, in other words, the application of the quantum theory to biology. We know that energy and matter are two aspects of a single phenomenon. And we understand, therefore, that the human body is as much energy (consisting of waves) as it is mass (consisting of solid particles). Surely the time. is ripe for a serious investigation into those healing methods that treat the body as energy rather than mass.

Treating the body as energy rather than mass is not a new idea. In China, for instance, the concept is as old as its culture. The basic purpose of acupuncture is to keep the energy of the body (known as *ch'i*) flowing freely. When this energy is blocked, disease sets in. The ancient Chinese also believed that this energy was to be found outside the body, as well. It was, in fact, the life force that governed the universe.

In the *Nei Ching*, the world's oldest book on medicine, said to be written more than 45 centuries ago, a physician named Koai Yu Chu describes " ... an essential, primordial energy that gives birth to all the elements and is integrated into them ... energy is only an abstract substance in the sky, whereas on earth it is transformed into a concrete physical substance." (Not only did he identify the unity of matter and energy thousands of years before Einstein, he also noted the existence of certain forces in space that have only recently been recognized by Western physicists.)

The Chinese *ch'i* is undoubtedly the same kind of energy – the energy that heals – to be discussed in different terminology throughout this book. For this power that man has been trying to harness throughout the centuries has a number of names: Hippocrates referred to a healing energy that flowed through all living things as the *vis medicatrix naturae*. It was called the *archaeus* by Paracelsus and animal magnetism by Anton Mesmer. It was the odic force of Baron Karl von Reichenbach and the vital force of Samuel Hahnemann. Wilhelm Reich names it orgone energy and D.D. Palmer, the Innate. It is the *ki* of the Japanese, the *prana* of the Hindus, the *mana* of the Polynesians, and the *orenda* of the American Indians. However, in spite of its many names, this elusive yet universal force always exhibits the same properties:

1. It can heal.
2. It penetrates everything.
3. It accompanies solar rays.
4. It has properties similar to other types of energy but is a distinct force unto itself.
5. It possesses polarity and can be reflected by mirrors.

6. It emanates from the human body and has been especially detectable at the fingertips and eyes.
7. It can be conducted by such media as metal wires and silk threads.
8. It can be stored inside inanimate materials such as water, wood, and stone.
9. It can fluctuate with weather conditions.
10. It can be controlled by mind.
11. It can cause things to happen at a distance, and enters into the dynamics of many paranormal phenomena.
12. It can be used for good or evil.

The Battle for Truth

Yet, despite its consistency, universality, and history, this force continues to be considered nonexistent by orthodox science. However, the battle for truth seems always to be waged against a storm of obstinacy. Galileo, imprisoned because he said the earth revolved around the sun, was afraid to discuss gravity as a universal force because the subject seemed 'occult.'

Fortunately, in this present era of antipragmatism, there is much room for hope. One must remember that before the isolation of electromagnetic waves, the concepts of both radio and television seemed mere fantasy. Now they are commonplace. It seems reasonable to assume that one day the healing energy will also become rooted in scientific fact. But it may take a while. After all, it took a considerable length of time to convince most people that the earth was round.

My own interest in this secret yet pervasive force was aroused two years ago when I wrote an article on psychic healing. Long unknown, or ignored by all but an esoteric few, psychic healing was just then forging its way into professional and even scientific circles. Today, those who continue to write the subject off as mere nonsense are coming to be regarded as anachronisms, close-minded hangers-on to the era of 'old-think.'

Part of my research involved an interview with Sally Hammond, author of *We Are All Healers*. After a scrupulous investigation of psychic healing all over the world, Miss Hammond deduced that the ability to heal psychically is probably innate in all humans, just waiting to be developed, provided one has the necessary compassion and willingness to acquire the required training, which involves the utilization of a special energy.

In fact, energy was the key word throughout my investigation of psychic healing. The healers that I interviewed usually described themselves as channels for an available energy. I was also informed that in England, psychic healers were awarded a certain credibility and respect by conventional physicians. "This is the way it should be," said one healer I talked with. "Physicians, psychiatrists, and psychic healers should work together. After all, to deny a whole field of study is to be unscientific. Energy is a fact. And one day the mind's energy will be able to be measured like everything else."

Spontaneous Healing

Donna Mastin, a teacher and resident of Southport, Ct., described a spontaneous healing after a car accident in which her vehicle was demolished. "My head went through the windshield, and it was a miracle that I wasn't killed. As it was, my forehead was a mass of cuts, and the nurses were unable to remove all the glass. Four days later I had a huge scab, which I covered with a wig in order to attend a Spiritual Frontiers meeting in Norwalk.

"The eight or ten people there did a healing meditation for me which included a 'laying on of hands.' This was at 9.30 p.m. At 10 p.m. my forehead started itching, and I jokingly remarked that maybe the healing had already begun. When I got home that night, there was no trace of the scab, and my forehead was completely clear. And I have witnesses to this event."

Again and again the people I interviewed would remark on this strange energy. An Episcopal priest, Father Dana Kennedy of Christ and Holy Trinity Episcopal Church in Westport, Ct., said: "We're all like little radio stations sending and receiving messages. This power, which we call energy, can be transmitted, and its flow is increased by real prayer. It is possible for human beings to tune in on something greater than themselves. Some call it energy; others call it God's presence."

"Although I've never witnessed an actual psychic healing," he continued, "I believe that human beings were created whole – a psyche and a body. And if the psyche is wounded, the body suffers, and vice versa."

Holistic Medicine

This concept of treating the body as a whole, the mind-spirit-body, seems to be a basic premise for those who deal with therapeutic energies. Holistic medicine, from the Greek word *holos*, is based on treating this mind-body-spirit — and the unifying factor is always energy.

My interest in this subject was further stimulated by a course offered at the New School for Social Research in New York during the spring of 1976. Introduced by Robert Giller, M.D., it was called 'Alternatives to Western Medicine: New Light on Therapeutic Energies.' The lectures all concerned treating the body as energy rather than mass, and included such subjects as orgone theory, psychic healing, acupuncture, chiropractic, and homoeopathy. These therapies had all intrigued me at one time or another, and most important, they all shared the common denominator of the healing energy.

Dr Giller's approach to medicine is holistic. He believes in treating the mind-body-spirit of a human being rather than his symptoms alone.

Giller's disappointment in Western medicine arose during his internship as he observed patients being treated as organs rather than total individuals. "One patient might see five different 'experts' who treated five different organs, but no one viewed the patient as a total entity," he said.

Uncomfortable with the idea of treating the symptoms of disease rather than its cause, Dr Giller became interested in preventive medicine. He also decided that he wanted to heal patients rather than treat diseases (prevention rather than pathology). It was this attitude that led him to the study of acupuncture and the concept of life energy. "I learned that the Chinese felt that there was a life force or vital energy that circulated through the body and that a balance or imbalance in this flow of energy determined health or disease. I also discovered that acupuncture, by the use of needles, rebalanced this imbalanced flow of energy."

Fascinated by the idea of a vital energy that heals, Dr Giller then discovered that the theory was at least 5,000 years old.

"When you read the history of medicine," he said, "it's the one concept that has survived all the way through. Every civilization and every culture has discussed the concept of life energy. This vital force which circulates through our bodies may be what determines life and death, health and disease.

"This life force is manifested in our body — in our heartbeat, our respiration rate, our metabolism, our acid-base balance.

"And to me, it's the same force that causes order in the universe; that causes the planets to circulate around the sun; that causes the change of seasons; that causes the tides; that causes, somewhere along the line, life itself."

In his practice of acupuncture, which began in 1974 after two years of study in England and Hong Kong, Giller became even more solidly entrenched in energy theories, and he is now writing a book on the subject.

Giller's purpose in presenting his course at the New School was to stimulate investigation of the body as energy rather than mass. "I hope to show that there is scientific validation that the body can now be viewed as a form of energy, and what that means in terms of health and disease. I believe there's a common essence to the cause of illness, its treatment and prevention, that is not currently recognized."

The common essence to which Giller refers is an imbalance in the flow of vital energy through the body, an imbalance that allows illness to set in.

The topics he covered at the New School seemed a diverse selection of therapies. But they were all connected to the energy theory. Most of the lecturers he chose were doctors on the staffs of medical schools. Although they are a small minority, the existence of this group portends well for the life-energy theory. The enthusiasm of the students, most of whom were interested in psychology and medicine, is also promising. The excitement in those classes was great, for the empirical evidence, as revealed by the lectures, pointing to the existence of a pervasive life force was compelling.

Drugs and Surgery

Life-energy advocates believe drugs and surgery to be radical healing measures and feel that their usage could be much minimized through the practice of preventive medicine. This theory would coincide with the proverbial Chinese classification of physicians into (a) superior (b) mediocre and (c) inferior. The superior doctor prevents disease; the mediocre doctor treats imminent disease before it manifests itself; and the inferior doctor treats actual disease. This would justify the ancient Chinese custom of one's paying the physician when in good health and withholding payment when ill.

There are, of course, situations where drugs and surgery will always be necessary. If one is hit by a car, suffers a severe infection, or requires an emergency operation, the medical care presently available can be lifesaving.

However, Thomas Kuhn in *The Structure of Scientific Revolutions* says that every dominant science eventually oversteps itself. Its very successes take it out to extreme positions and practices that hasten its fall and eventual replacement by another approach.

In medical science, a new approach would not offer a replacement but a complement – evolution, not revolution. And healing energy theories that have persisted since the dawn of civilization should be explored, not ignored, even when they seem to venture into the domain of psychic phenomena. We have learned from modern physics that matter disintegrates into energy and that energy dissolves into changing patterns of something still unknown. This unknown something may well be related to the psyche or mind.

Before the quantum theory was formulated, it was thought that one could have a purely objective picture of nature – that there were things moving here and there, completely unaffected by the scientist's gaze. Today, physicists recognize that when they make an observation, they disturb the system. The consciousness of the observer himself must now be considered. It is possible that we live in an invisible and intelligent ocean of energy that penetrates and interpenetrates our body cells. The question is: can we learn to control it?

Philosophy has decreed that the only constant is change. Therefore, as scientific knowledge, especially in physics, expands to include new realities, so must our concepts of the universe, the earth, and the human body also be enlarged.

There are few challenges greater than that of harnessing the healing energy and forcing it into the realm of fact. It is small wonder that this hope, which has the strength of centuries behind it, seems to have added momentum as it continues to haunt innovative thinkers today. For if this energy can be verified, much of our philosophy, religion, and science will be revolutionized – in quantum leaps. The blending of physics and metaphysics, which is already occurring, will be completed, and many miracles will no longer seem absurd. Certain psychic phenomena will be revealed as simple manifestations of natural law. And the recurrent dream of both ancients and moderns will prove to be well founded in the stuff that truth is made of.

2

THE SECRET OF THE HUNA

The earliest mention of the healing energy comes to us from a period of prehistory. The ancient *kahunas,* priests who settled in Hawaii, called it *mana,* and their system for using it was referred to as the *huna.* In this era, nature and supernature were one. *Mana* was considered a simple fact of magic, and there were no microscopes or sceptics to deny its existence.

My introduction to this subject was through a book called *The Secret Science Behind Miracles* by Max Freedom Long. It was a book that I picked up at 10 p.m. and finally put down at 5 a.m. with a feeling that can best be described as awe. For an entire week I looked at the world with new eyes, subliminally hooked, so to speak, on the *huna,* which might be portrayed as a workable system of psycho-religion that can produce what we commonly refer to as magic.

My enchantment, however, was short-lived, for when I discussed the *huna* with friends, it was difficult to make the theory sound rational. In fact, it was intimated that the charming eccentricity that had once been mine might be deteriorating into something more serious if I could indeed provide even lip service to such patent nonsense. Advised to read Descartes in order to regain my senses, I did – and found that the crusty old father of Western logic had pursued his own career in response to a dream.

So much for common sense. It was, after all, uncommon sense that concerned me, and the *kahunas* apparently had possessed it. In any event, while my friends pursued their conventional wisdom and 'normalcy,' which they did not find incompatible with nightly excursions into the world of television sitcom, I delved deeper into 'magic.' And my fascination, I felt, was justified when I later heard Dr

Robert Jeffries of Westport, Ct., a scientist, inventor, and professor, describe the *huna* as "the most internally consistent, comprehensive metaphysical philosophy that exists."

How to Make Miracles Happen

The word *huna* means secret. And the word *kahuna* means keeper of the secret. The secret referred to is the knowledge of how to make miracles happen, whether in healing or everyday living.

No one is sure where the *kahunas* originated. Speculation has included their connection with early astronauts and lost continents. Their history has been handed down to us orally, and legends naturally vary. Max Freedom Long's research led him to believe that the first *kahunas* were members of 12 ancient tribes who lived in the Sahara Desert while it was still green and lush. When it became arid, they moved to Egypt, where, according to Long, their secrets may have been used to help build the pyramids and provide the roots of the various mystery religions. Eventually, due to fear of repression, they left Egypt and settled in Hawaii, although one tribe is said to have returned to Africa, where it settled in the Atlas Mountains.

The *kahunas*, unfortunately, were always few in number, and their psychic wisdom, through time, eventually became less universal in its scope. What continued, however, at least in Hawaii, was a system of workable 'magic' (miracle cures, weather control, influence over animals, firewalking, prognostication, etc.) that was practised until the arrival of Christian missionaries.

The missionaries perceived the *huna* as black magic, and the practice was banned. But although officially against the law, it continued to flourish privately. Officials rarely enforced punishment when a functioning *kahuna* was exposed because they were afraid to provoke his wrath. For the power or *mana* used by the *kahunas* can be used to harm as well as to heal. The *huna* is, however, vigorously opposed to injuring any individual; and the system has been used, 99 per cent of the time, for the good of humanity. It was, unfortunately, the aberrant one per cent for which it became famous in the early part of the 20th century. This was largely due to an internationally renowned play called *Bird of Paradise*, that sensationalized the *kahuna* death prayer, which is a quite chilling and effective phenomenon.

When Max Freedom Long arrived in Hawaii in 1917, he became intrigued by what he heard about the *kahunas*. He interviewed the highly respected scientist, William Tufts Brigham, who had for some time been curator of the Bishop Museum in Honolulu. (Brigham appears in the American *Who's Who*, 1922-23.) According to Long, Brigham believed in the authenticity of the *huna* system and had kept careful records of incidents that described healings, weather control, walking on hot coals, calling sharks to the beach, and other extraordinary happenings.

But although Brigham accepted the validity of the *kahunas'* feats, he had no idea how they occurred. He tried to solve the mystery of the *huna* until his death in 1921. Long then took up the task, and after years of study, arrived at some answers based on his examination of the Hawaiian dictionary. The secret of the system, he felt, was revealed through the definitions of certain words. It was in the language, Long believed, that he discovered the truth.

The effectiveness of the *huna*, he said, is based on a profound knowledge of nature, both human and other. The *kahunas* are both expert psychologists and masters of natural science. The result is the material that miracles are made of.

Three Selves

Essential to the successful working of the system is the premise that each individual possesses three selves (or spirits): the first is the high self, a kind of all-knowing god self; the second is the middle self, which would correspond to our conscious will; and the third is the low self, the primitive self that controls appetites and desires. These three selves might be compared to the psychological definitions of superconscious, conscious, and subconscious.

Each of these three selves contains its own second body, an etheric body; and each of the three second bodies has its own distinct type of power.

According to Long, there are actually ten elements to understand in the *huna* system:

1. Low self or subconscious. This self remembers but cannot reason; it is located in the solar plexus; its Hawaiian name is *unihipili*.

2. Middle self or conscious. This self cannot remember but has full reasoning power; it corresponds to the left hemisphere of the brain, and its Hawaiian name is *uhane*.

3. High self or superconscious. It knows the past, the present, and as much of the future as has been planned, created, or projected on its level; it acts as an overself or parental guardian angel; it corresponds

to the right hemisphere of the brain, and its Hawaiian name is *aumakua*.

4. Etheric body of the low self. Though invisible, it is dense and sticks to whatever we touch; when removed from the contact, it draws out a long invisible thread from itself that connects one with the thing contacted in a form of semipermanent union. It is not known how permanent this thread or the main body itself may be, but it seems to survive far longer than dense physical substances.

All things were supposed by the *kahunas* to have a shadowy body, be they crystals, plants, animals, fabricated articles, men and even thoughts. This substance is a conductor of vital electrical force or currents, and can be used as a storage place for same. When heavily charged with the low voltage of the force, it becomes rigid and firm enough to be used as a 'hand' or instrument to move or affect physical objects, as in table tipping. The Hawaiian name is *kino aka*.

5. Etheric body of the middle self. It is not sticky and does not pull out into threads. Its Hawaiian name is also *kino aka*. It is a conductor of middle-voltage *mana* that is used in thinking and will; it also forms the ghostly body in which the spirit functions after death.

6. Etheric body of the high self. The Hawaiian name is, again, *kino aka*. This provides the residence of the high self, and seldom makes contact with the physical body. In many respects it resembles the etheric bodies of the two lower selves.

7. Energy used by the etheric body of the low self. This consists of a low-voltage electrical force that can flow over sticky threads described in number 4; it can carry chemical substances with it as it flows from person to person; it can take the form of magnetism, and can be stored in porous substances such as wood; a large discharge of this low-voltage vital force, commanded by the will (of the middle self) can exert a mesmeric effect. Its Hawaiian name is *mana*.

8. Energy used by the etheric body of the middle self. This is responsible for thinking and willing activities. Used as will, it can be mesmeric, provided that a thought form is introduced into the mind of the subject. It cannot travel over the shadowy substance threads, as can the lower voltage. Its Hawaiian name is *mana mana*.

9. Energy used by the etheric body of the high self. This is a high voltage of vital force – of atom-smashing voltage; it creates miracles; its Hawaiian name is *mana loa*.

10. The physical body that houses the three selves is known in Hawaiian as *kino*.

The magic attributed to the *kahunas* is based on the idea of the three selves and their ability to manipulate the energy (or *mana*) of their three etheric bodies.

In order to accomplish this, obviously, the three selves must be in communication with one another. The middle self, which is the most familiar since it controls our conscious actions during waking hours, cannot communicate directly with either the high self or the low self. (It can, however, contact the low self through the use of the pendulum, hypnosis, and dreams, all of which will be discussed later.)

Essential to the system is that the high self and the low self are able to 'talk' to one another regularly. In other words, subconscious and superconscious are in touch with one another without the conscious being aware of it. When a *kahuna* wants something to happen, he appeals to the lower self, which then contacts the higher self.

Enid Hoffman, author of *The Huna, A Beginner's Guide*, describes this process:

"The low self, seated in the solar plexus, sends its messages to the middle self via the reticular activating system (RAS), a cone-shaped complex of nerves radiating from the brain stem and flaring up in a fountainlike display of nerve fibres that penetrate every part of the brain. The RAS is called the 'doorkeeper to consciousness.' All the information we get from the low self is channelled through it.

"The low self is continually sending messages to the high self through the RAS, but these messages bypass our conscious awareness as long as we are centred in the middle self. The messages to the high self are limited by the programming in the low self. And the middle self can reach the high self only through the low self. So one of our main objectives in the huna is to remove the limitations on what can be sent to that higher brain, the right hemisphere of the cortex.

"Increasing the activity of the right hemisphere is a major aim in becoming a kahuna, for it is in this part of the brain that higher concepts are understood and creative thought takes place. The high self can reveal to us relationships that we might never see otherwise; it can create larger patterns that include information stored in our memory banks. If you wish the high self to assist you in accomplishing your desires, 'ask and you shall receive.' The high self sees your life as a whole and the interrelationships of all events within it. The high self, however, can manifest itself only through the right hemisphere of the brain, and that can be activated only by energy sent by the low self."

The Brain's Two Hemispheres

Before investigating the *huna*, I, like most people, was aware that the brain consisted of two hemispheres. I also knew that the right one controlled the left side of the body and vice versa. But I had not realized that the left hemisphere of the brain was the reasoning factor, responsible for the rational, logical part of our thinking, and that the right hemisphere was the domain of what we call intuitive thought or higher consciousness.

If, as the *huna* suggests, our higher self 'resides' in the right side of our brain and the middle self in the left side, the implications of this concept become quite interesting. For it occurs to one that the consciousness expansion brought about by meditation and certain drugs might well be due to the activation of this frequently unused right hemisphere.

A book with the formidable title of *The Origin of Consciousness in the Breakdown of the Bicameral Mind* by Julian Jaynes also deals with this subject. The author suggests that homo sapiens was originally bicameral (two- chambered) in the sense that the right hemisphere of the brain spoke to the left, and the left heard and obeyed. In other words, the right hemisphere told (through voices) the left hemisphere what to do. These voices, even though they came from within, were assumed to belong to higher beings or gods. According to Jaynes, it was these voices that directed the construction of the pyramids.

Schizophrenics, according to the book, are the closest among modern humans to these early 'preconscious' men because they also hear voices. Among bicameral men, of course, the situation was considered normal. It might be said that people at that time were in direct communication with their gods.

The breakdown of the bicameral system, Jaynes says, occurred sometime before 1000 B.C. The written word especially caused the left (reasoning) hemisphere of the brain to become more active. Eventually, through disuse, the right hemisphere stopped speaking, and man no longer had access to its advice.

Perhaps the consciousness expansion we are now experiencing in the Aquarian age is, in a sense, man's attempt to reclaim his gods – through the reactivation of the brain's right hemisphere.

One of the primary goals of modern *huna* students is to bring both hemispheres of the brain into optimum working efficiency.

Carl Jung wrote: "In the exploration of the unconscious we come upon very strange things, from which a rationalist turns away with horror, claiming afterward that he did not see anything. The irrational fullness of life has taught me never to discard anything, even when it goes against all our theories (so short-lived at best) or otherwise admits of no immediate explanation."

Jung's statements are especially applicable to the comparisons of the three selves.

Long stressed that the three selves, although belonging to the same body, were totally independent of one another and could become separated. And he felt that when they did become separated, the result was often what we call mental illness. In fact, Long believed that the best case for the *kahuna* theory of the three selves and their energy bodies was to be found in comparing multiple personality cases with obsessional insanity or schizophrenia.

"In the first (multiple personality)," he writes, "the patient remains sane because he or she is obsessed or controlled by a normal ghostly intruder who has his own subconscious and conscious selves, and who can, therefore, both remember and use reason."

(It was mentioned earlier that the low self can remember but not reason and the middle self can reason but not remember. Long's use of the term ghostly intruder refers to an entity possessing both high self and low self.)

"Only personality (conscious self) may change, or only memories (subconscious self) may change, or both may change — and still there is sanity because a reasoning conscious self is always in control of the body regardless of changes."

In the second case (obsessional insanity or schizophrenia), he writes, "insanity results from the changes because the conscious self is displaced and a new one does not take over the body. This leaves the resident subconscious in charge, and, lacking reason, it keeps the body alive but in a condition of lack-of-reason, or insanity. Or, an invading subconscious self may obsess or take over the body after the resident two selves have been driven out.

Cases of insanity are common in which a foreign subconscious self obsesses a body. We know that it is foreign because it brings with it a foreign set of memories and convictions, even when illogical. The insane who believe themselves to be Napoleons are of this type, often not dangerous, often being able to remember from day to day, but never able to use the type of reason characteristic of the conscious self."

There are some readers who will cringe at the idea of various selves wandering about the globe — middles and lows joined or separate. But if one considers the ordinary statement, "He has lost his sanity," just *what* is the sanity? Is it his complex of rational beliefs, or is it his middle self? Because the *huna* is so practical, psychological terms can nearly always be substituted for those that seem metaphysical.

The *kahunas,* as a matter of fact, were aware of complexes and fixed beliefs long before they came to the attention of Freud. Dealing with the guilt complex that might be held by the subconscious or low self was an integral part of their system. It was the guilt complex, for instance, that might make the low self vulnerable to an invading 'ghostly intruder.' And the removal of this guilt complex played a crucial role in *kahuna* healing.

Dr Brigham studied a number of cases that illustrated the *huna* system at work in the realm of instant healing. One of the least complicated accounts among his records is the following, as reported by Long:

"My close and trusted friend, J.A.K. Combs, of Honolulu, who is a fellow student of *kahuna* lore, and who has given me much invaluable aid, had for a grandmother-in-law one of the most powerful women *kahunas* in the [Hawaiian] Islands. She loved Combs and told him many things about her secret knowledge, her power, and her practices. On the occasion in question, Combs attended a beach party at her country home. Many guests had arrived when a car drove up to the edge of the beach and several Hawaiians got out. Among them was a man who was slightly intoxicated. He missed his step from car to soft sand and fell. As he fell, there was the characteristic snapping sound of breaking bones.

"Inspection showed a compound fracture of the left leg just above the ankle. The bone ends pressed visibly out against the skin. Combs, who had heard the familiar sound of breaking bones and had himself suffered such a break, realized the seriousness of the injury and proposed that the man be taken at once to Honolulu for treatment, but the elderly *kahuna* arrived on the scene and took over. Kneeling beside the injured man, she straightened the foot and leg, pressing on the place where the ends of the broken bones pushed out the skin, and then began a low chanted prayer for healing. In a short time she fell silent. Those who stood about watching tensely could see nothing until her hands suddenly moved slightly on the man's leg, and she took them away, saying quietly in Hawaiian, 'The healing is finished. Stand up. You can walk.'

"The injured man, now entirely sobered, rose wonderingly to his feet, took a step, and then another. The healing was complete and perfect. The leg showed no indication of the break in any way."

The *kahunas* explain instant healing as a process that involves the high self and its energy, *mana loa*. This was described previously as the highest voltage of vital force and that which is used in all miracles.

Also involved in the case above were the flesh, bone, and blood of the injured limb and the etheric or second body of the patient — particularly the part of it that duplicated the broken section of the leg.

The *kahunas* believe that the second body of the low self (the etheric double) provides a mould for the body's shape and all its cells. In order to mend a broken leg, the high self dissolves the injured bone and other tissues into ectoplasm, this usually being invisible, but not always. As the etheric body mould is made of invisible substance, it cannot be broken or injured. Thus, with the mould of the normal leg, there available, the ectoplasmic material of the dissolved parts is resolidified in the mould, with the result that the healing is instant and the limb is restored to its former condition.

This explanation, according to Long, applies equally to all healing in which abnormal conditions of deformity or disease prevail. "If there is a cancer," he writes, "it is changed to ectoplasmic substance and then made into normal tissue to fill the mould of that part of the body as it was before the cancer developed."

This process is what is commonly referred to as dematerialization and materialization. Dematerialization, according to Alfred Stelter, author of *PSI Healing*, means "a dissolution of organic matter, which probably turns into a fundamentally new state or energy beyond the four states of the material world — solid, liquid, gas, and plasma. This form must be much more subtle than atoms — perhaps similar to elementary particles — and quasi-nonelectrical, so that it can easily penetrate solid material structures. Assuming that bioplasma is involved, as postulated by the Russian researchers Inyushin and Sergeyev, dematerialization would be the transition of normal organic substance into bioplasma. Rematerialization or simply materialization is used to designate the return or transfer of bioplasma to normal material condition."

Materialization and dematerialization are considered impossible by most scientists because the transformation of matter into energy and then back again into matter would require the same kind of enormous energy as that released in a nuclear bomb. Or the same kind of enormous energy the *kahunas* ascribe to *mana loa*.

Religion usually attributes miracle healings to God or a saint or the Christ power, and the cures accomplished at shrines such as Lourdes certainly attest to this premise. However, the percentage of success among the *kahunas*, according to Long, has been much higher.

Before examining the methods by which the average person may get in touch with his low and high selves, the *kahunas'* attitude toward guilt complexes should be more fully discussed.

According to Long, the complex or fixation of ideas was referred to by one *kahuna* as the "thing eating inside." It is a belief or conviction held by the low self and may or may not be correct. Once lodged in the memory of the low self, it is difficult both to find and remove.

The *kahunas* were, however, more successful than modern psychologists in dealing with such fixations because they understood the value of suggestion accompanied by a physical stimulus.

"The low self," writes Long, "is so accustomed to having the middle self think of imaginary things that anything resembling an imagining is paid scant attention. The low self is best impressed by REAL AND TANGIBLE THINGS. For instance, the water used in religious ceremonies to 'wash away sins' is something tangible, and therefore impressive to the low self. The *kahunas* have used water in ceremonial washing of the patient while giving the spoken suggestion that all sins are being washed away. They have used many other physical stimuli – for perhaps 10,000 years."

Phineas Quimby, who will be mentioned in Chapter 5, described three pillars upon which his healing was based: suggestion, *rapport*, and an unknown energy. Quimby, as we shall see, developed his technique after much practice. He would first pray to what he called the wisdom; after contact was made, he became aware of a tremendous force, which he called the power. This was the unknown energy to which he referred, and it was usually effective in healings. Sometimes, however, his patients would not respond, and Quimby, after much thought, decided that this was due to their own deep-seated beliefs or guilt complexes.

In order to dissolve the complexes, Quimby appealed to his patients' religious beliefs. God, he told them, was perfect; therefore, how could He have created anything imperfect; all illnesses must be, then, mere figments of the imagination. With all imperfect things rendered unreal, the disease-causing guilt complexes seemed to dissolve. Although this may sound illogical, it apparently worked. According to the *huna* logic, Quimby was cleansing both the middle and low selves of deep-rooted fixations in order to effect cures.

In fact, the ability to harm a person through magic was thought by the *kahunas* to depend upon the victim's deep sense of guilt, caused by wrongs done others. It was such a guilt sense or complex that made the subconscious of the victim vulnerable to attack from the "malicious animal magnetism" that so terrified Mary Baker Eddy, the founder of Christian Science, to be discussed in Chapter 5.

Hawaiian Death Prayer

During the first half of the 20th century, the Hawaiian death prayer received a great deal of notoriety throughout the world, primarily due to the aforementioned play, *Bird of Paradise*. Max Freedom Long, interested in pursuing the truth of this matter, checked medical data, interviewed doctors, and arrived at the conclusion that one or two patients at the Queens Hospital in Honolulu died in this way each year.

After years of investigation, Long believed that he finally understood how the death prayer worked. The *kahunas*, as we know, were convinced that each individual had three selves, or spirits, and that the low self, or subconscious spirit, was vulnerable to hypnosis.

Long writes: "To become able to use the 'death prayer' a *kahuna* must inherit from another *kahuna* one or more ghostly subconscious spirits. (Or he might, if sufficiently psychic, locate subconscious spirits or ghosts, and use hypnotic suggestion to capture and enslave them.)"

According to Long, in very early Hawaii, prisoners of war or other unfortunates were sometimes given what apparently was a very potent hypnotic suggestion to cause their subconscious spirits, after death, to separate themselves from their conscious spirits and remain as ghosts to guard sacred stone enclosures or native temples. It is probable, writes Long, that some of these unfortunates were given orders to serve *kahunas* in the 'death prayer' magic after they were executed.

A *kahuna*, in order to use the death prayer effectively, must have at least one, usually two or three, of these captive ghost or subconscious spirits. When he wished to kill someone, the *kahuna* would summon his enslaved spirits and issue hypnotic directions. These included orders to absorb *mana* from food and drink especially prepared by the *kahuna*. The *mana* or vital force, says Long, was undoubtedly transferred from the body of the *kahuna* into food, drink, and ceremonial objects such as small white stones and certain pieces of wood.

"The spirits were also given very definite instructions as to what they were to do with the force," Long writes. "They were to catch the scent from a bit of hair or soiled garment belonging to the intended victim, and follow it much as a dog does a track. Upon reaching the victim, they were to await their chance to enter his or her body. This they were able to do because of the power to use as a paralyzing shock the surcharge of vital force given them by their master. The order which the spirits were trained to obey was recorded in one case. It was:

'O Lono,
Listen to my voice.
This is the plan:
Rush upon _____ and enter;
Enter and curl up;
Curl up and straighten out."

This process of "curling up and straightening out" involved the spirits entering the body of the intended victim and taking away his *mana* or vital force; this caused his death, usually within three days. The symptoms displayed by a death prayer victim were always the same. A numbness, which started in the feet, eventually made its way to the heart.

"When the death had been accomplished," writes Long, "the spirits left the body, taking with them their great charges of vital force, and returned to their masters. If the victim had been rescued by another *kahuna*, and the spirits sent back by him to their owner with hypnotic orders to attack their master, they might make such an attack with fatal results. In order to avoid such a danger, a magic ritual of cleansing was usually performed by the *kahuna* sending out the spirits (*kala*). Or, as was most often the case, the person who had hired the *kahuna* to send the 'death prayer' to another, and who had vouched for the fact that the intended victim deserved such drastic punishment, would be named as the one responsible and to be attacked should another *kahuna* send the spirits back before their task was accomplished."

After a successful mission, the *kahuna* instructed his captive spirits to 'play' until they had used up the extra *mana* taken from their victim.

This play, according to Long, often took the form of what some people call poltergeist activities. The spirits would move or throw objects, make loud noises, and create a bedlam of some proportions. (Several years ago I investigated similar occurrences in Bridgeport, Ct., when a young girl was said to be involved with poltergeist activities. The happenings were witnessed by a number of people who simply could not believe their eyes as they reportedly observed furniture fly through the air. The incidents were later attributed to mass hypnosis or imagination. The affair was hushed up and soon forgotten.)

It must be remembered that the death prayer of the *kahunas* was rarely employed. The *huna* magic was used, nearly always, to aid, not annihilate. Strongly integrated into the system, in fact, was the supremely ethical notion that the worst sin of all was to harm another human being.

According to Long, the *kahunas* were able to prevent sharks in Hawaiian waters from attacking human beings. In all the years he lived on the islands he never heard of anyone being killed by sharks that were considered man-eaters elsewhere.

Through their 'magic,' the *kahunas* were allegedly able to make contact with the sharks' high selves and thus create a pact of good will. According to Long, this frequently resulted in close relationships between human beings and individual sharks:

"Families were often intimately associated with the various creatures, and made magical pacts with their guardian high selves. This gave rise to a form of totemism in which certain rites were observed, and the totem beast of the family was not eaten by that family.

"Children and the high selves who watch over the lower creatures seem to have a strong affinity ... In Hawaii there is a strong belief that human baby spirits may, under certain circumstances, be born into the bodies of small sharks and thus keep up the totem relations between sharks and the shark-families of the humans."

The *Geographic News Bulletin* of December 10, 1934, described a ritual where children chanted in order to make contact with the high selves that control the sharks and turtles. The procedure, known as calling the shark and the turtle, took place at the village of Vai Togi, Samoa.

"The native children and adults gathered for the ceremony, then the children were sent alone to a point of land jutting over the sea. There they recited an old legend telling how a prince and princess had been changed to a shark and turtle respectively. As they chanted they beckoned. In about five minutes a small shark four or five feet long appeared in the clear water beyond the breaking waves, swam around in plain sight for about a minute, and then departed. Soon a turtle appeared in a like manner, remained for a short time, and swam back to deep water."

Reaching the Low Self Through Hypnosis

No one really understands hypnosis or why it works. It is loosely defined as a state of heightened suggestibility induced by another person, or, in some cases, by the individual himself. The hypnotic state is usually achieved through bodily relaxation accompanied by concentration on a narrow range of stimuli. It is a practice that dates back to antiquity, where it was used as a religious-magical technique among the Babylonians, Egyptians, and Greeks.

My own introduction to hypnosis occurred about 15 years ago when a psychologist put me into a light trance and suggested that I evoke happiness images. The first was that of myself reading in a large panelled study lined with books. The window was open, and the room was filled with the smells of burning leaves and certain indefinable odours that I attach to autumn. The second image was that of myself wafting about someone's garden at a summer cocktail party. Perhaps I did not need hypnosis to conclude that reading all day and partying all night would make me happy. Nonetheless, those images were very clear and have never faded – nor has my respect for hypnosis.

According to the *huna* interpretation, my lower self was telling me something important. For hypnosis very definitely allows the low self free expression. In fact, one of the greatest values of hypnosis may be to allow the low self or subconscious a means of telling us what we really want or need.

Although the trance state has been studied for over two centuries, it continues to be an enigma. There are many theories, of course, but none that provides any full explanation. Hypnosis, we know, is not the same as sleep, although studies indicate that it is closer to light sleep than to either the waking state or deep slumber. The famous physiologist, Dr Ivan Pavlov, believed it to be a state of brain inhibition related to sleep but limited to inhibition of motor impulses. Others have suggested that certain centres in the brain are activated by suggestion. The psychological theories seek to explain hypnosis in terms of an expansion of autosuggestion into heterosuggestion, sexual submission to the hypnotist, identification with the hypnotist's presumed omnipotence, or regression to a primitive level of functioning. In spite of its wide use, hypnosis has retained a certain occult-tainted image and is still frowned upon by some orthodox scientists.

Nevertheless, its applications in general medicine are almost limitless. It is used to relieve anxiety and stress in more ailments than one can name: hypertension, Raynaud's disease, coronary disorders, heart palpitations, cerebral accidents, asthma, speech disorders, and a host of others, not to mention its alleviating influence in the relief of pain.

Hypnosis has been of great help to me personally during bouts with anxiety and insomnia. The hypnotist I call upon is named Ben Sandoval, who has been practising hypnosis for more than 23 years. Although he works therapeutically with insomniacs, worriers, drug addicts, smokers, and over-eaters, Mr Sandoval's great passion is with psychic phenomena. His special forte, he says, is to develop mediumship in psychically evolved subjects, and he has now collected over 100,000 feet of taped messages resulting from 'interplane communication.' The age-regression experiments of those in hypnotic trance have reportedly brought Mr Sandoval into contact with former Roman emperors, 'lost' Atlanteans, Egyptian priestesses, and others. Mr Sandoval's technique is to hypnotize the mediums in order that they may summon the appropriate guides, and then tape their messages.

I have observed Mr Sandoval age-regress about ten subjects, and I remain unconvinced of the phenomenon's validity. It seemed to me that there may have been as much drawing upon imagination as incarnation. However, what *is* imagination? And who knows what esoteric messages have been programmed into our subconscious minds? Certainly, it is unjust to write the whole thing off as nonsense as it is to accept it without question.

Of one thing we can be sure. Hypnosis is and will continue to be an excellent means of communicating with the low self.

Reaching the Low Self Through Dreams

Dreams, like hypnosis, are still a mystery. No one seems to know what they are, although the theories are endless. They have been described as a reflection of reality, a source of divination, repressed hostilities and desires, manifestations of the collective unconscious, or, as the *huna* suggests, a means for the low self to communicate with the high self.

The notion that dreams predict the future is as old as history. Egyptian dream interpretations are recorded from the 12th Dynasty (1991–1786 B.C.). In India a document called *Atharvaveda*, attributed to the fifth century B.C., contains a chapter on dream omens. A Babylonian dream guide was discovered in the ruins of the city of Nineveh among tablets from the library of the emperor Ashurbanipal (668–627 B.C.). The Old Testament is filled with prophetic dreams. And among pre-Islamic peoples, dream divination was so powerful a force that it was finally banned by Muhammad.

Ancient literature abounds with 'message' dreams, in which a god appears to the dreamer during times of difficulty and tells him what to do. In the 19th century, Joseph Smith, founder of the Mormon religion, said that an angel had directed him to the location of buried golden tablets that described American Indians as descendants of the tribes of Israel.

The Eskimos of Hudson Bay and the Patani Malay people believe that during sleep one's soul leaves his body to live in a special dream world, and he must not be wakened lest his soul be lost.

In Borneo, there is a tradition that if a man dreams that his wife is an adulteress, her father must take her back.

A Paraguayan Indian, after dreaming that a missionary shot at him, tried to kill the missionary on the following day.

In classical Greece, dreams were connected with healing. The sick went to sleep in oracular temples, and their dreams were interpreted curatively by the priests. It was believed that the god or goddess at whose altar the patient slept was responsible for sending the dream after he or she (the deity) had become convinced of the petitioner's devotion. The individual, upon awakening, would then describe the dream to the priest, who offered the therapeutic interpretation. Many patients were convinced that their healings took place during the dream itself.

The *kahunas'* explanation for such phenomena was that the gods and goddesses so petitioned were really the higher selves of the supplicants. M.F. Long suggests that altars, shrines, and sacred relics act as physical stimuli in aiding the petitioners to make workable prayers for healing; and since it was only through such workable prayers that the high selves could be summoned, such stimuli may be indispensable in the process of many miracle healings.

Long describes the healing that takes place at shrines by the following: One or more normal departed spirits (each having its low and middle selves united to make them normal) elect to remain at the shrine and do all they can to help heal those who come asking for healing. These normal spirits will have learned to call on their high selves and can persuade them to heal instantly or in a matter of a few hours — or even as long as three days (as recorded at Lourdes). Many come to pray, making what may be considered a 'circle' of value similar to gatherings at spiritualistic seances. The normal spirits are supplied with vital force by the living; so also are the high selves. When anyone who is free of guilt fixations, and who has faith, is able to make a good thought-form picture of the desired condition (healing), and is also able to make telepathic contact with the normal spirits, and (1) through them with a high self, or (2) without their aid contact their own high selves directly, the miracle of healing results.

The most commonly accepted diagnoses of what dreams are spring from psychology. Freud believed that dreams offered the bridge to the unconscious, home of repressed sex and hostility. Jung, however, saw dreams in a somewhat larger light. He believed they were an expression of the collective unconscious of the race as well as the personal unconscious of the individual. And he believed them to be guides to future thoughts and actions, not mere reflections of unresolved personal conflicts.

Jung remarked in 1928: "Dreams may give expression to ineluctable truths, to philosophical pronouncements, illusions, wild fantasies ... anticipations, irrational experiences, even telepathic visions and heaven knows what besides."

He believed that the insights achieved through dreams brought the dreamer to a level of self-understanding that would be impossible during waking life.

"Within each of us," said Jung, "there is another we do not know. He speaks to us in dreams and tells us how differently he sees us from how we see ourselves. When we find ourselves in an insolubly difficult situation, this stranger in us can sometimes show us a light which is more suited that anything else to change our attitude fundamentally; namely, just that attitude which has led us into the difficult situation."

Jung apparently believed that dreams were attempts to solve problems. The *kahunas* believed that dreams *could* solve problems.

We see, then, that from antiquity dreams have been viewed as a source of divination; or as a form of reality; or as a healing force; or as an extension of the waking state. Psychoanalytic theorists, aside from Jungians, continue to, for the most part, follow Freudian edicts. And modern research focuses on efforts to discover complex biochemical and neurophysiological bases of dreaming. There are, too, many who agree with the philosopher Bertrand Russell, who said: "It is obviously possible that what we call waking life may be only an unusual and persistent nightmare." As with hypnosis, no single theory is yet available.

The *huna* attitude toward dreams, as interpreted by Enid Hoffman, suggests that the low self at this time is trying to integrate all the incompleted activities of the day into the personality and to tie in these experiences with incomplete past experiences. The purpose, apparently, is to form some kind of intelligible pattern. The low self also uses dreams in an effort to influence future events.

Dreams, Miss Hoffman says, are dramatic productions written and staged by the low self. And whatever we do not deal with in our waking hours provides the raw material.

Huna students, she adds, use dreams in three ways: first, they recall and record their dreams. This is done by keeping a pad and pen by the bedside along with a nightly message to the low self; one must also state a wish to remember the dream.

Second, the student must analyze his dreams. This brings the conflicts that the low self has been grappling with alone to the conscious, middle-self surface. When enough material has accumulated in the dream log, a definite pattern should emerge.

Third, they programme their dreams to solve problems. This is best accomplished, says Miss Hoffman, by the following: "Just before retiring, (1) fill a drinking glass with water; (2) review the problem to be solved; (3) drink half the water, holding the problem in your mind; and (4) give your low self instructions to work on the problem and send up a solution as you drink the rest of the water the next morning." (The *kahunas* considered water their symbol for *mana*.)

It is an intriguing concept that our dreams actually can be made to work for us. In her book, *Dream Power,* Dr Ann Faraday describes the Senoi tribe of the Malay Peninsula and its attitude towards dreams. These people, who are known as the most democratic group in anthropological records, with no crime for hundreds of years, are profoundly influenced by both the interpretation and manipulation of dreams. According to the Senoi, all dream images are fragments of the personality and consist of psychic forces disguised in external forms. Children are taught to confront the bad spirits of nightmares in order to master them. They are also instructed to surrender to falling dreams so that they may turn into flying dreams. The flying dreamer then somehow programmes his 'trip' to be constructive, and he returns to the waking state with new knowledge from afar.

The resemblance between the dream body of the Senoi and the etheric body of the *kahunas* is quite striking, as is their mutual wish to harness the dream force.

Sleep, according to the *huna*, offers an ideal time for one's low self to be given suggestions. A record, with a list of directions, might be started automatically several hours after retiring. The low self will hear the words and turn them into thought forms. These are then lodged in its etheric body where they remain impervious to the usual rationalizing process of the middle self upon awakening.

Reaching the Low Self with the Pendulum

One of the easiest ways to achieve contact with the low self is through the use of the pendulum. Although this device has been used for centuries by priests, kings, and scientists, my first experience with it was through a game of extrasensory perception. This consisted of a board, which included the letters of the alphabet, the words YES and NO, plus the pendulum itself, a small transparent ball made of plastic attached to a chain. When I held the pendulum above the diagram and asked it questions, it moved either vertically for YES or horizontally for NO. The most incredible thing about the process was that it appeared to move of its own free will. I *knew* that I was not consciously manipulating its swing.

Half believing that I had made contact with some strange esoteric force, I spent about six hours asking it all kinds of questions, most of which could be answered yes or no. Using the alphabet to spell out words was a slower and more confused process, although I did have some rather provocative replies. When I asked the pendulum who was directing it, for instance, it spelled GOD.

Most of the questions I asked were those about which I had definite opinions. And I realized, eventually, after many of its predictions had not come true, that the pendulum was responding the way I *wanted* it to. Still, the fact remained that I had not *consciously* willed its movements. At that time, long before I became acquainted with the *huna*, contacting my low self or subconscious, which is, of course, what I was doing, did not seem to hold any particular value; so I abandoned the practice.

It was, therefore, with great interest that I learned from Enid Hoffman's book that the pendulum holds much importance for students of the *huna*. Learning how the low self or subconscious thinks and feels is, after all, a matter of no small consequence. By asking the right questions, the middle self is able to root out deep-seated fixations and complexes held by the low self. Queries such as: Do you think it's wrong to make money? Do you want to remain married? Do you enjoy being a parent? may bring some surprising replies and be tremendously instructive insofar as one's true feelings are concerned.

A pendulum can be constructed from almost anything – a ring, pendant, bead, button, or other weight suspended from a length of thread, twine, or chain; and there are many more sophisticated versions. The instrument moves in five different directions: vertically (yes), horizontally (no), clockwise (good), counterclockwise (bad), and diagonally (maybe). These motions vary according to the individual, but it is my understanding that most positive reactions are either vertical or clockwise and vice versa. The Rev Hannah Kroeger, of Boulder, Colo., who uses her pendulum to choose the right foods, reports in her pamphlet, *The Pendulum, The Bible and Your Survival*, that each individual has his own pendulum swing and should not be influenced by those who say that it must move clockwise for positive and vice versa. Beginners can discover their own positive pattern, for example, by holding the pendulum and thinking or saying aloud the word yes over and over again. When this has been established, the same can be done for the negative pattern, substituting, of course, the word no.

The pendulum, aside from its use to gain contact with the subconscious, has almost more applications than one can mention. Locating the site of disease, the choosing of food – decisions of all kinds. According to pendulum devotees, the possibilities of this device are endless.

Before leaving the *huna* and its system of selves, energies, and etheric bodies, I would like to quote a few passages from George Meek's book, *From Enigma to Science*. Mr Meek, after years of research and communication with scientists, offers a section called the A.B.C.'s of Metascience, in which he lists alphabetically certain postulates regarding human beings and their relationship to the universe. Some of these are so remarkably consistent with the *huna* that it seemed no mere coincidence that I happened on Mr Meek's book just after reading Max Freedom Long.

From the A.B.C.'s of Metascience: "The physical or material body, composed as it is of just certain of the elements of the periodic table, is in the lowest range of the vibrational frequencies spanned by man's several vibrational systems.

"Man's conscious, subconscious, and superconscious minds; his memory; and the portions referred to as soul or spirit, may each involve a separate but intermingling energy field or system of vibrational nature, each with its own frequency range. (It seems to be a good speculation that one or more of these vibrational systems involves a type or types of energy as of now unknown, and/or outside our present concept of the electromagnetic spectrum.)

"The formation of the physical body, its repair and maintenance, and the replenishment of its cells, appears to be the result of the operation of the energy field system of the next higher level of vibration. This vibrational 'body' has been called the etheric or the bioplasmic."

While under the spell of the *huna* 'magic,' I found myself repeatedly finding correlations between its tenets and those described elsewhere (in at least one hundred books dealing with the paranormal, for example). Words changed, definitions varied, but the principles were the same.

The *mana* is probably the oldest known name for the healing energy; and one day we may find that the ancient *kahunas*, with their ethical system of psychoreligion, knew the answers to questions that most of us have barely begun to ask.

3

THE FOUNDERS OF HOLISTIC MEDICINE: PYTHAGORAS AND HIPPOCRATES

The true father of Hellenic medicine, preceding Hippocrates by at least a century, was Pythagoras, who was born about 580 B.C. Although well-known as a philosopher, mathematician, and astronomer, Pythagoras was also a physician, and he considered healing the noblest of all pursuits. It was integrated into his investigation of ethics, mind, and soul, as well as his desire to make a rational science of metaphysics.

Pythagoras's name for the healing energy was *pneuma*. The *pneuma,* he said, came from a central fire in the universe and provided man not only with his vitality but his immortal soul. Pythagoras's central fire was a primordial force, the sparks from which gave life to man.

Unlike other energy seekers, Pythagoras did not have to worry about *proving* his concepts to a dubious scientific community, primarily because the medical institutions of ancient Greece were religious as well as philosophic. But his genius did, apparently, arouse an envious wrath that eventually proved fatal.

Born on the Greek island of Samos, Pythagoras arrived at his philosophy (he is said to have invented that word), by studying with the wisest men of many countries: Egypt, Chaldea, Persia, Arabia, India, Babylonia, and Palestine-Phoenicia. He studied the nature of the soul with the Brahmans; he learned the inner traditions of Moses from the rabbis; and it was probably from the magi that he learned mathematics, music, astronomy, and the remedies for many diseases.

Regarded as a kind of prophet, Pythagoras was considered by many to possess actual divinity. According to legend, his parents visited the famous Pythian oracle at Delphi before his birth and were told that their son would be extraordinary. The oracle was presumed to be founded by the god Apollo, after he had slain the grisly female dragon known as Python, who was terrorizing the community; and the name Pythagoras means mouthpiece of the Pythian oracle. The oracle functioned through a medium similar to those who exist today: a middle-aged woman would go into trance, make contact with Apollo, and then answer her petitioner's questions, many of which were doubtless concerned with health.

The rumour that Pythagoras might be the son of Apollo through a kind of virgin birth was enhanced by the fact that he was tall, handsome, and 'golden.'

Since Pythagoras preferred speaking to writing, most of his ideas, like those of Jesus and Buddha, come to us through his disciples. Historians agree, however, that he was a great teacher who believed his purpose in life was to clarify the true meaning of existence, which he felt to be the evolution of the human spirit: men must advance themselves morally and intellectually through right living, right thinking, and a constantly seeking mind.

Transmigration of Souls

At the heart of his philosophy was a belief in the transmigration of souls. He said that souls must assume physical bodies in order to function and learn on the earth plane; and the way he lives in one plane will determine the individual's (or the soul's) existence on the next. Pythagoras's theory of transmigration of souls, unlike other reincarnation beliefs, includes the possibility of rebirth as animals.

The souls, Pythagoras believed, came from the previously mentioned central fire existing in the centre of the universe. The central fire, he said, was the first cause of creation and was fragmented throughout the universe as warm vapours or 'hot *pneuma,*' which produced souls.

After 30 years of travel, when he was about 50, Pythagoras established his famous academy in Crotona, which at that time, 529 B.C., was already famous as a health resort. His students, all carefully chosen, were advised to begin each day with meditation, and there were many exercises for purification of mind and strengthening of will. The curriculum included harmony, music, the dance, gymnastics, proper diet, mathematics, and astronomy. The harmony achieved through music, dance, and numbers, he believed, was imperative to the health of both body and soul.

His contributions to mathematics and astronomy are well known. Some say that Pythagoras believed health to be a proper mathematical relationship in the parts or elements of the body. Even the soul had a number. He was the first to call the earth round, and he gave the name 'Kosmos' to describe it.

He said that the universe was an intelligent, living sphere; and he believed human beings to be conscious parts of a universal, vital, constantly changing process – a kind of cosmic dance of evolving souls.

Physical health was, according to Pythagoras, integrally related with the well-being of the mind and spirit. In this respect we can easily consider him the founder of holistic medicine. The human body, in fact, was simply, to Pythagoras, a vehicle for the soul to advance and shed ignorance. The spirit, trapped in matter, must learn through intellect and discipline how to tame the irrational tendencies of its human nature.

Golden Verses

Because he recognized the importance of free will, Pythagoras was often indirect in his advice to students. His rather cryptic way of presenting important truths is exemplified by his famous Golden Verses. Some of these, as listed in *Pythagoras,* by Thomas Stanley, are:

Verses XIII-XVI: "Observe justice in all your actions and words; neither use yourself, in any manner, to act without reason. But always make this reflection, that it is ordained by destiny for all men to die; and that the goods of fortune are uncertain; and that, as they may be acquired, they may likewise be lost."

Verses XVII-XX: "Support with patience your lot, be it what it will, and never repine at it; but endeavour what you can to remedy it. And consider that fate does not send the greatest portion of these misfortunes to good men."

Verses XL-XLIV: "Never suffer sleep, to close your eyelids, after going to bed – till you have examined by reason, all your actions of the day. Wherein have I done amiss? What have I done? What have I omitted that I ought to have done? If in this examination, you find that you have done amiss, reprimand yourself severely for it, and if you have done any good, rejoice."

Verses LIX-LX read, "Likewise know, that men draw upon themselves their own misfortunes voluntarily, and of their own free choice, wretches as they are! They neither see, nor understand, that their good is near them. There are very few of them who know how to deliver themselves out of their misfortunes. Such is the fate that blinds mankind, and takes away their senses. Like huge cylinders, they roll to and fro, always oppressed with ills without number. For fatal contention is innate in them and pursuing them everywhere, tosses them up and down, nor do they perceive it. Instead of provoking and stirring it up, they ought to be yielding to avoid it."

One of the most revolutionary aspects of Pythagoras's school was the admission of women. For in that era, even those who were not actual slaves were regarded with much scorn. As one popular poet of the day phrased it: "There are only two happy days a wife offers her husband – the one when she weds and the one when she dies."

The First Known Feminist

That Pythagoras believed in equal opportunity for both sexes made him a maverick of the highest order. Two centuries later, Plato (who was much influenced by Pythagoras) also pleaded for equality for women in his *Republic*; but Pythagoras was the first known feminist. His female students, known as the Pythagorean women, were greatly honoured throughout Greece as the finest examples of their sex.

It was inevitable that Pythagoras and his students, so highly trained in virtue and knowledge, would eventually offer themselves as guardians of the state. And although no one knows exactly how he died, most historians agree that Pythagoras and many of his disciples were slaughtered by enraged political rivals.

It is ironic that this legendary Greek embodied the most futuristic concepts of holistic medicine – for he combined body, mind, and spirit with a system of metaphysics that gave meaning not only to life but after-life.

Hippocrates, the ancient Greek known to us as 'the father of medicine,' believed in a healing energy, which he called the *vis medicatrix naturae* (the healing power of nature). In any cure, he said, this energy is the principal healer, and all the physician can do is remove or reduce the impediments to the proper flow of this vital force.

Hippocrates advised his students that the first law of healing was: "Above all, don't make things worse!" He believed in using drugs sparingly and only when absolutely necessary; in his time, there were only 268 known drugs, most of which were simple herbal concoctions.

The truth is that Hippocratic treatment was largely a form of holistic, preventive medicine in its basic state: "Live a healthy life," Hippocrates advised, "and you are not likely to fall ill, except through epidemic or accident. If you do fall ill, proper regimen will give you the best chance of recovery."

Although most of our knowledge concerning Hippocrates's life is somewhat cloudy, based mainly on the writings of Plato and Meno, it is generally agreed that he was born in 460 B.C. on the island of Cos. The descendant of eminent physicians, he received his first medical instruction from his father.

After travelling widely throughout Thrace, Thessaly, Asia Minor, and the island of Thasus, he taught medicine at Cos and died a very old man in Thessaly.

Hippocrates, like Pythagoras, said that health depended on keeping the body in balance. He believed in the proper harmony of blood, phlegm, black bile, and yellow bile. As one or another of these juices (or humours) predominated, the individual would be sanguine, phlegmatic, choleric, or melancholy. Unless these four juices were blending properly, disease would set in.

Health, he said, would be restored when the internal heat of the body (fever) actually cooked the juices. After this, there follows a crisis and elimination of the superfluous substance. The elements may then be restored to a state of equilibrium by the *vis medicatrix naturae*. It was faith in this force that led Hippocrates to adopt an expectant attitude in the treatment of many of his cases. He abstained nearly always from surgical interference and prescribed drugs as mere aids to nature in the expulsion of the morbid matter after a fever crisis.

Disease was, according to Hippocrates, often the body's attempt to re-establish its harmony. In other words, illness was, in a sense, beneficial, and to interfere with its symptoms was not usually a good idea. Nature, he said, is the healer of disease.

The Hippocratic Collection

Hippocrates and his followers wrote many excellent reports on all branches of medicine. The treatises, about 60 in number, are known as the Hippocratic Collection or the *Corpus Hippocraticum*. The *Corpus* includes text-books for physicians, counsels for laymen, lectures for students, reports of researches and observations, clinical records of interesting cases, and essays by Sophists interested in the philosophical aspects of medicine.

It is impossible to know which books in the collection were actually authored by Hippocrates himself. There are ten books on anatomy and physiology; ten on general physiology; two books on dietetics; ten on general pathology; eight on surgery, including some on purely spinal surgery; one on ophthalmology; ten on gynecology; and some books on obstetrics and pediatrics.

In his quest for the healing energy, Hippocrates is said to have advocated strongly the practice of what we today call chiropractic. This came as a great surprise to me, since I had always believed that therapy to have been invented rather recently by a man named Palmer.

However, according to Dr Kleanthes A. Ligeros of Greece, in his book, *How Ancient Healing Governs Modern Therapeutics,* Hippocrates advised his students to study closely the purpose and structure of the spinal functions. Referring to that section of the Hippocratic Corpus which deals with joints, Dr Ligeros says that Hippocrates understood the nervous system and its influence upon the whole body.

Hippocrates and his successors are recognized as the first rational physicians because they released medicine from religion and philosophy. Occasionally they advised prayer as an adjunct, but the overall thrust of the Hippocratic Collection is towards objective therapy. The Hippocratics insisted that treatment must proceed by careful observation and accurate recording of specific cases and facts. Diseases, they said, had natural causes; and those physicians who attributed illness to demons and gods were charlatans and quacks.

There can be no doubt that Hippocrates elevated his profession in the matter of ethics, and this is readily apparent in the content of his oath. Again, we cannot be sure that Hippocrates wrote this famous essay. There are those who say he did and those who say he didn't. But one likes to think that he did.

The Hippocratic Oath

"I swear by Apollo the healer, by Aesculapius, by health and all the powers of healing, and call to witness all the gods and goddesses that I may keep this oath and promise to the best of my ability and judgment.

"I will pay the same respect to my master in the science as to my parents and share my life with him and pay all my debts to him. I will regard his sons as my brothers and teach them the science, if they desire to learn it, without fee or contract. I will hand on precepts, lectures and all other learning to my sons, to those of my master and to those pupils duly apprenticed and sworn, and to none other.

"I will use my power to help the sick to the best of my ability and judgment; I will abstain from harming or wronging any man by it.

"I will not give a fatal draught to anyone if I am asked, nor will I suggest any such thing. Neither will I give a woman means to procure an abortion.

"I will be chaste and religious in my life and in my practice.

"I will not cut, even for the stone, but I will leave such procedures to the practitioners of that craft.

"Whenever I go into a house, I will go to help the sick and never with the intention of doing harm or injury. I will not abuse my position to indulge in sexual contacts with the bodies of women or of men, whether they be freemen or slaves.

"Whatever I see or hear, professionally or privately, which ought not to be divulged, I will keep secret and tell no one.

"If, therefore, I observe this oath and do not violate it, may I prosper both in my life and in my profession earning good repute among all men for all time. If I transgress and forswear this oath, may my lot be otherwise."

In the first line of the oath, Aesculapius, the legendary god of healing, is invoked. At that time, temple-hospitals throughout Greece flourished in his name. Called Asklepeiads, these were actually health centres of preventive medicine. Dieting, baths, exercises, massage, and even psychotherapy were practiced by healers who were also priests. Dream interpretation, as mentioned in Chapter 2, was considered important in revealing to patients the secret longings that might be making them ill. And this was theorized 23 centuries before Freud and Jung.

For a long while, Hippocrates was said to be connected with the Asklepeiad cult, but more recent historians say no. Hippocrates died, they say, before the Asklepeion temple was built in Cos. And besides, they add, Hippocrates was too rational to have been associated with healers who were also priests.

In spite of Hippocrates's search for the healing energy, we must look at him as one of the first to lead medicine into its present mechanistic mode. By separating science from religion and philosophy, he may have severed the former from its wellsprings of inspirational or intuitive knowledge. For Greek science was the child of Greek philosophy. And Greek philosophy was the child of Greek religion. And in the beginning, the three were whole, and they were certainly used holistically by Pythagoras.

Mechanistic and Intuitional Perception

The two types of thinking, mechanistic and intuitional, were of major concern to Henri Bergson, the French philosopher (1859-1913) who was known (erroneously) as the father of the life force, or *élan vital*. (His proposal that the whole evolutionary process should be seen as the endurance of an *élan vital* that is continually developing and generating new forms dates back to the Greek philosophers, especially Heracleitus.) In his *Introduction to Metaphysics*, written in 1913, Bergson describes the two modes of perception:

"Evolution is creative, not mechanistic. There are two profoundly different ways of knowing. One reaches its furthest development in science; is analytic, spatializing, and conceptualizing, tending to see things as solid and discontinuous. The other is an intuition that is global, immediate, reaching into the heart of a thing by sympathy. The first is useful for getting things done, for acting on the world, but it fails to reach the essential reality of things precisely because it leaves out duration and its perpetual flux, which is inexpressible and to be grasped only by intuition."

We find echoes of Bergson in astronaut Edgar Mitchell, one of few to personally experience the true heights, both literally and figuratively, of modern technology. While viewing earth from outer space, Mitchell found his respect for the mechanistic science that had placed him there to be profound. But more profound still was the subjective or what he called religious knowledge that overwhelmed him with the larger reality of the universe. In the introduction to his book, *Psychic Exploration*, he urges the merging of subjective and objective reasoning; of science and religion; of reason and intuition.

The healing energy will be finally harnessed by a holistic mind that can blend the mechanistic with the inspirational. This requires a mentality that can master the discipline and order of the mechanistic as well as approach the inspirational in an intelligent and organized way. The mechanistic mentality has been responsible for the centuries of observation and careful analysis that have led to modern science; and this approach continues to be of great importance to 20th-century man.

However, we live in an age where the mechanistic intelligence can complement and work with the intuitive. One factor without the other is incomplete: mechanism without intuition leads to sterility; and intuition without mechanism leads to a lack of discipline that renders it ineffectual in a material world. Both types of thinking, like two halves of a whole, must be incorporated. In Pythagoras, of course, they were. But without the rationalism of Hippocrates, medical science could never have advanced as it has. In the evolution of ideas, perhaps it is inevitable that there be an emphasis upon first one type of thinking and then the other before the two can blend into an ideal marriage of thought.

Throughout history there have been men who seemed to combine the two intellects. Galen was one of these. He was also the most important advocate of the healing energy after Hippocrates and before Paracelsus. Born in Turkey in 129 A.D., Galen achieved great acclaim as both philosopher and physician.

Galen believed that a vital energy or spirit pervaded and activated every organ of the body. And like Pythagoras, he referred to this force as *pneuma*. Many physicians at that time, as they do today, considered the body as a kind of machine. Galen objected to this premise wholeheartedly, and said that whereas a machine is merely the sum of its parts, an organism implies the purposeful control of the parts by the whole. This purposeful control of *pneuma,* he said, explains the origin, structure, and functions not only of the human body but of the universe as well.

Galen, continuing the holistic concepts of Hippocrates and Pythagoras, obviously believed in the unity (body-mind-spirit) of the human organism.

His contributions to anatomy were enormous. According to Will Durant's *Story of Civilization,* Vol. III, he described accurately the bones of the cranium and the spinal column, the muscular system, the heart, and the glands. He proved that the arteries contain blood, not air as the Alexandrian school had taught for 400 years. He founded neurology, and was so skilled in symptomatology that he often diagnosed without questioning the patient.

Although Galen's life and medical discoveries are no less valuable than those that follow, he is mentioned here primarily as a bridge between Hippocrates and Paracelsus.

Most pertinent to our subject was his belief in the *pneuma,* which gave rise to the vitalist school of medicine championed throughout the centuries by such men as George Ernst Stahl (1660-1734); Dr

Friedrich Hoffman (1660-1742); John Hunter (1728-1793); and two 19th-century biochemists, Liebig and Wohler.

It would be impossible to describe the careers and theories of all these men in one book. Their names are presented, however, in order to emphasize the consistency with which energy concepts arise. All of the vitalists believed that the functions of the human body and its environment were controlled by a mysterious force that they called the vital principle. According to our premise, this vital principle is the same power that the *kahunas* called *mana*, that Pythagoras called *pneuma,* and that Hippocrates termed the *vis medicatrix naturae* — four different names for the phenomenon known throughout the ages as the energy that heals.

4

PARACELSUS

One of the most brilliant, outrageous, innovative, and original physicians the world has ever known was a little man with a large head named Paracelsus. He believed in a healing energy that radiates within and around man like a luminous sphere. This force, which he called *archaeus,* could operate at a distance and was able both to cause and cure disease.

He also said that the stars and other bodies, especially magnets, could influence man by means of this force, which pervades all space. It was this theory that became known as the magnetic or sympathetic system of medicine, which is the basis for magnetic healing.

Born near the village of Einsiedeln (now in Switzerland) on November 10, 1493, Paracelsus's real name was Philippus Aureolus Theophrastus Bombastus von Hohenheim. And it is from the tempestuous nature of his personality that we derive our word bombastic. At an early age, he decided to follow his father in the professions of medicine and chemistry. From childhood he had been an avid observer of plants, minerals, and metals; Paracelsus was always fascinated by what he described as the secrets of nature.

Shortly after graduating from medical school, he renamed himself Paracelsus, which means above or beyond Celsus, for he believed himself to be greater than the famous first-century medical philosopher who was known by that name. His self-confidence was justified, for Paracelsus combined the mysticism of Pythagoras and the rationalism of Hippocrates with a genius of his own that led him to an investigation of alchemy with all its related 'magic' which he consistently attributed to natural science.

This red-faced, balding, and occasionally heavy-drinking man who cursed his fellow physicians and delighted his students gave to the world some of medicine's highest achievements. His contributions to the understanding of diseases like syphilis, silicosis, and goitre are outstanding, not to mention the advances he made in the healing of wounds. He might also be considered an early champion of homoeopathy, for he was known to say that, if given in small doses, "what makes a man ill also cures him."

Carl Gustaf Jung, the psychiatrist, said: "We see in Paracelsus not only a pioneer in the domains of chemical medicine, but also in those of an empirical psychological healing science."

Sidereal or Star Body

Of compelling interest today is Paracelsus's early concept of man's second body, what he called the sidereal or star body. He was certain that man has two bodies: the animal, flesh-and-blood one and the sidereal (or star or astral) one. The animal body, he said, was elemental and housed the lower instincts; the astral was the originator of art, wisdom, and the higher instincts. Both were parts of mortal man, and both were subject to disease. He also spoke of the third immortal body, which was a kind of eternal spark or soul; but it is the second body, as vulnerable to illness as the first, with which we are here concerned.

Many psychics have long believed that the human body is inter-penetrated by another body of energy that gives off a glow known to most as the aura. The respected medium, Eileen Garrett, states in her book, *Awareness*: "Throughout my whole life, I have been aware of the fact that everyone possesses a second body – a double. The double is a distinct fact in Eastern and theosophical teaching, and as such, it is said to be an energy body, a magnetic area associated with the physical human corpus, an area in which the immaterial forces of the cosmos, the solar system, the planet, and one's more immediate environment are normally transformed in the life and belief of the individual."

Is this second body or etheric double the medium of telepathic and clairvoyant projection? Does it offer an explanation for psychic healing? Is it related to the middle self of the *kahunas*? Does it indeed exist?

In his bestseller, *Life After Life*, Raymond A. Moody, Jr., M.D., reports that people who were declared clinically dead often describe the existence of a second body. Dr Moody writes: "I have heard this new body described in many different terms, but one may readily see that much the same idea is being formulated in each case. Words and phrases which have been used by various subjects include a mist, a cloud, smoke-like, a vapour, transparent, a cloud of colours, wispy, an energy pattern and others which express similar meanings."

Through the use of Kirlian high-frequency photography, Russian scientists have reportedly also seen this second body in plants, animals, and humans.

According to *Psychic Discoveries Behind the Iron Curtain* by Ostrander and Schroeder, the Russians describe it as "some sort of elementary plasma-like constellation made of ionized, excited electrons, protons and possibly other particles ... But at the same time, this energy body is not just particles. It is not a chaotic system. It's a whole unified organism in itself."

In fact, it has now been nearly a decade since a group of doctors in the Soviet Union announced that all living things have two different bodies: one made of atoms and molecules and a second made of energy. Their name for this second body is the biological plasma body, bioplasma for short. And this bioplasma, they say, does not exist merely in the body. It permeates all of space.

If this second body of energy does exist – and we may call it sidereal, astral, orgonic, or bioplasmic – its medical applications would be revolutionary. Healing this second body might be easier and safer than working on the physical body. One would indeed be treating the body as energy rather than mass.

Paracelsus often identified his *archaeus* with the etheric double of the physical self. And although it motivated the material body, was in fact its power, it could be influenced by the thought and actions of the mind. Negative thoughts, he asserted, could block the flow of the *archaeus* and give rise to disease.

The Quest for Truth

Paracelsus, not unlike our other energy seekers, possessed genius, infuriated his peers, and was on fire with the quest for truth. And although his mind was supremely logical, he often said, "Resolute imagination can accomplish all things." He believed that one attained knowledge through both intuition and experience. To neglect either of these two methods would, he said, lead to disaster. Intuitive reasoning, which he knew to be most commonly ignored, was, he believed, guided by the all-pervasive force, *archaeus.*

In order to make his point and outrage his peers, Paracelsus frequently remarked: "Magic is a great hidden wisdom, and reason is a great open folly." Because he lived in an era when science had not yet become mechanized and due to his reputation for miracle cures, his 'magic' and alchemy were not dismissed out of hand.

He travelled in Egypt, Arabia, Palestine, and Constantinople. Everywhere he studied alchemy in order to discover the latent forces of nature and how to use them. He also attended many prestigious medical schools and wondered how "the high colleges managed to produce so many high asses."

"The universities," he said, "do not teach all things, so a doctor must seek out old wives, gypsies, herb women, monks, and peasants and take lessons from them. A doctor must be a traveller, for knowledge is experience."

Because of his fame as a healer, Paracelsus was appointed town physician in Basel, where he also lectured at the university. Unfortunately, he scandalized the populace by publicly burning the books of other physicians and attacking mercilessly the medical practices of his time. In explaining why he had become a medical reformer he said: "Since I saw that the (present) doctrine accomplished nothing but the making of corpses, deaths, murder, deformity, cripples, and decay, and had no foundation, I was compelled to pursue the truth in another way, to seek another basis, which I have attained after hard labour."

According to Kenneth Walker's *Story of Medicine,* Paracelsus said: "The best of our popular physicians are the ones who do the least harm. But unfortunately, some poison their patients with mercury, and others purge or bleed them to death. There are some who have learned so much that their learning has driven out all common sense, and there are others who care a great deal more for their own profit than for the health of their patients. ... A physician should be the servant of nature, not her enemy; he should be able to guide and direct her in her struggle for life, and not throw, by his unreasonable influence, fresh obstacles in the way of recovery."

Paracelsus believed alchemy to be the chemistry of life, dealing with the very processes of existence. And in spite of his reputation for sorcery, one has the impression that he used his alchemic kitchen primarily for the preparation of medicines.

The Homunculus

And yet ... there is an intriguing report that Paracelsus actually managed to produce that phenomenon known as the homunculus. In alchemical language, the homunculus is the 'son of wisdom' or the *lapis philosophorum* (philosopher's stone). And according to Webster's dictionary, the homunculus is "a manikin that is artificially produced in a curcurbit by an alchemist." (A curcurbit is a vessel used for transmutation.) The homunculus allegedly constructed by Paracelsus was a tiny man made from horse dung, human sperm, chemicals, and, of course, magic. This miniature human being was presumably developed and kept in a glass bottle.

Awed observers claimed to have seen Paracelsus dancing in his garden and communing with spirits as he gathered dew for his medicinal concoctions. Enemies announced that his various miracle cures were the result of his having made a pact with the devil. He was, however, beloved by all the many patients who had benefited from his ministrations.

Part of Paracelsus's therapeutic success was undoubtedly due to his understanding of the healing energy. According to *The Mystical and Medical Philosophy of Paracelsus,* by Manly P. Hall, Paracelsus's healing philosophy was founded upon his quest for adequate ways of conducting energy into the human body, setting up poles for its reception and distribution, and removing impediments to its circulation. He recognized the importance of proper nutrition, and believed food to be more than a mere physical substance.

The body was, Paracelsus said, a medium for the transmission of the *archaeus*, or life force. "Several plants," he adds, "growing in the same soil will develop differently according to their natures. Some will have red blossoms, and others white. Some will have fragrance, and others have no odour, or possibly an objectionable one. It is the nature of the plant that determines what it takes from the soil, and it is the nature of Man that determines what he will derive from universal nutrition. But this energy will help all things to grow according to their kind and constitutions. Man possesses the power to change certain parts of himself. He can become more noble or more kindly. He can engage in activities which strengthen him, or he can neglect his needs and thus diminish his proper powers."

Paracelsus believed that all bodies had their roots in atmosphere or space. "They derive their nutrition from an invisible field of substances," writes Hall, "which is an intangible kind of earth. Thus the universe is an inverted garden, with its roots in space. This intangible atmosphere is the source of all elements and substances, and the nutritive agent which maintains the living processes. It is also the root of intelligence and emotion, and the source of certain archetypes or patterns by which species are differentiated. Various kinds of energy can be released only through creatures or beings in whose natures appropriate sympathetic polarities exist. Man's uniqueness lies in the fact that within him are poles capable of attracting countless forms of energy. Therefore, man is capable of knowing everything necessary to his own survival. He can attain to all necessary ends because the roots and seeds of universal achievements are within him.

"Actually, however, on the level of function, man responds only to such energies as he can capture and hold by those polarities which he has strengthened and developed by skill and thoughtfulness. Such polarities can be of many kinds, such as mineral, nutritional, astral, psychical, emotional, mental, and spiritual. For example, an individual can never energize an emotional power which is inconsistent with the development of his own emotional nature. If, therefore, he hates, he cannot create the archetype of love by which he will participate in this noble emotion, unless he changes his own way of life. Man is always in the midst of energies, many of which are beyond his conscious understanding. Yet, gradually, through the growth of his own mind, he attains to true learning, and becomes responsive to the universal energies which sustain learning and help it to increase."

Prelude to Psychology

It should be remembered that alchemy was then regarded far more than a mere chemical science. It was also a philosophy. Not only were base metals to be turned into gold; alchemy also concerned the transmutation of the soul. Carl Jung considered it a prelude to psychology, a key to the collective unconscious, and he has written many fine essays on the subject.

Paracelsus did indeed sound part-alchemist, part-psychologist when he wrote: "To be an alchemist is to understand the chemistry of life. Medicine is not merely a science but an art; it does not consist in compounding pills and plasters and drugs of all kinds, but it deals with the processes of life, which must be understood before they can be guided. A powerful will may cure, where a doubt will end in failure. The character of the physician may act more powerfully upon the patient than all the drugs employed."

Because of his vicious invective against fellow physicians, Paracelsus was forced to flee Basel in 1528. For years, he wandered and wrote. In 1536 he made a great comeback with a book on surgery. In 1541, at the age of 48, he took up an appointment under the prince-archbishop, Duke Ernst of Bavaria. This was also the year that he died, and the circumstances of his death were mysterious. Historians agree that he dined sumptuously that last evening at the White Horse Inn in Salzburg. But afterwards, nobody knows exactly just what did occur. Some say that Paracelsus drank too much and had a stroke. Others believe that he was poisoned and then thrown over a cliff by a group of jealous doctors.

Within his coarse exterior, Paracelsus was himself a kind of alchemical mixture of doctor, metaphysician, and even poet.

"Man is a star," he said. "Even as he imagines himself to be, such he is. He is what he imagines ... Man is a sun and a moon and a heaven filled with stars ... Imagination is creative power. Medicine uses imagination strongly fixed. Fantasy is not imagination, but the frontier of folly ... Because man does not imagine perfectly at all times, arts and sciences are uncertain, though, in fact, they are certain and, by means of imagination, can give true results. Imagination takes precedence over all."

History has given Paracelsus a great deal of credit for his contributions to modern medicine. Not included, however, are his concepts of the healing energy, or 'the second body.' And although he is credited with the founding of magnetic healing, that system has yet to be regarded with any particular esteem. It was, however, the foundation for the medical theories and vitriolic career of Franz Mesmer.

5

OTHER ENERGY SEEKERS: FRANZ ANTON MESMER, BARON VON REICHENBACH, PHINEAS QUIMBY, AND EDGAR CAYCE

Franz Anton Mesmer (1733-1815) was convinced, like Paracelsus, that human beings were influenced by a subtle force in the universe that could be harnessed for healing purposes. He said that "the sun, moon and fixed stars mutually affect each other in their orbits; that they cause and direct on earth a flux and a reflux, not only in the sea, but in the atmosphere; that they influence in a similar manner all organized bodies by means of a mobile fluid, which pervades the whole universe and draws all things together in mutual intercourse and harmony."

Mesmer was impressed by the notion that Paracelsus had captured these forces through the use of minerals that had acted as magnets. He was further influenced by the Flemish chemist, Jan Baptista van Helmont (1577-1644), who believed that magnetic fluids radiated from the human body and could be focused on the minds and bodies of other people through an act of will.

Like Paracelsus and van Helmont, Mesmer assumed that the human body was inherently polarized into positive and negative; if this polarity could be combined with that of the universal healing energy, or fluid, the resulting power could be harnessed to cure the ill.

Although he received his medical degree in 1766 from the University of Vienna, it was not until seven years later that Mesmer postulated his theory of animal magnetism, which was his name for the healing energy. He believed health to be based on the free flow of this energy, or vital fluid, throughout the body, with disease setting in when it was blocked. (We should remember that Paracelsus believed disease to be caused by blockages in the flow of *archaeus*.)

Metallic Magnets

Mesmer came to the conclusion that this vital force could be attracted and applied through the use of metallic magnets. He discovered that when he passed magnets over his ailing patients, they appeared to get better. The magnets, he believed, attracted the healing energy from the universe, transmitted it to his patients, and revitalized them.

Aside from his cures, a number of influences aided his theory. New discoveries were being made in electricity and magnetism. In England an entertainer named James Graham became interested in Benjamin Franklin's experiments. He opened a temple of health, where his clients bathed in electrically magnetized water, which they said cured their ailments.

In America a doctor named Elisha Perkins invented a pair of brass and copper tractors that he said drew pain and other ills from the body. (George Washington was one of the first to use this device.) A priest named (oddly enough) Father Maxmilian Hell was using magnets to cure disease, and Mesmer had witnessed at least one of his demonstrations.

After a number of cures through the use of magnets, Mesmer discovered that he didn't need them. Whether he had become sufficiently magnetized to heal without them or was simply a natural channel for the energy, one does not know. His 'miracle' cures infuriated other doctors, and he was ordered to appear before the faculty of medicine in Vienna to explain his techniques. After observing his demonstration, the physicians accused him of practising magic. He was expelled from the Austrian medical association and forced to flee the country.

Group Sessions

In Paris, more liberal than Vienna, Mesmer was able to set up a highly successful practice. In fact, his patients became so numerous that he was forced to have group sessions. This was accomplished through his use of a 'bacquet,' a huge tub filled with diluted sulphuric acid. Iron bars protruded from the apparatus in order to strengthen the magnetizing process.

His patients sat in a closed circle around the bacquet holding hands, and the rods were applied to the painful parts of their anatomy. Mesmer, dressed in a long lavender gown and carrying a kind of wand, walked about the room touching each individual. This process, he said, stimulated the flow of animal magnetism to a point where the patients reached a kind of convulsive crisis that was crucial to their care.

This kind of behaviour apparently enhanced his reputation, for all of Paris was agog. His clients were drawn from the upper ranks of society, and there can be little doubt that they gained help from his methods.

Mesmer's perception of animal magnetism was probably best described by one of his pupils, a Dr D'Eslon. In Westlake's *The Pattern of Health,* this appears as follows:

1. Animal magnetism is a universal, continuous fluid, constituting an absolute plenum in nature, and the medium of all mutual influence between interstellar bodies and between the earth and animal bodies.

2. It is the most subtle fluid in nature, capable of flux and reflux, of ebb and flow; of receiving, propagating and continuing all kinds of motion.

3. The human body has poles and other properties analogous to the magnet.

4. The action and virtue of animal magnetism may be communicated from one body to another, whether animate or inanimate.

5. It operates at a great distance without the intervention of any body.

6. It is increased and reflected by mirrors, communicated, propagated and increased by sound , and may be accumulated, concentrated and transported.

Although Mesmer was adored by Parisian socialites, he was detested by Parisian doctors. In 1784, King Louis XVI appointed a commission of scientists and physicians to investigate animal magnetism. The commission included Benjamin Franklin and the illustrious French chemist, Antoine Lavoisier.

In spite of the overwhelming evidence in favour of Mesmer and his very real 'miracle' cures, the commission unanimously agreed that animal magnetism was a hoax. Mesmer's healing energy, they said, was nonexistent, and his success with patients was due simply to the influence of individual imagination.

The French doctors also sent a secret report to the king warning that the crisis so important in Mesmer's cures − a point at which the disease reached its climax and some patients fell into convulsions − might become hereditary and cause an epidemic. They also said that Mesmer's female patients ran the constant risk of being seduced by him. Mesmer was thereby branded a lecher as well as a fraud.

Although thoroughly discredited and called "the biggest quack of the 18th century," Mesmer managed to live out the rest of his life peacefully, and he died at a ripe old age.

Discoverer of Hypnosis

Ironically, Mesmer is incorrectly credited with the founding of hypnosis. It was actually discovered quite by accident by one of his disciples, the Marquis de Puysegur, during a session of magnetic healing.

The Marquis, delighted by the way Mesmer's techniques brought about a somnambulistic state, was further elated when he found that certain individuals placed in that state appeared to become clairvoyant, or able to see beyond one's normal perception. More exciting still was that many of those in the clairvoyant phase were able to diagnose diseases. This was how mesmerism gave rise to mental healing, psychic phenomena, organized spiritualism, and, eventually, Christian Science.

Mesmerism became known as hypnosis in the latter part of the 19th century when James Braid, a British surgeon, re-examined the procedure and attributed it to psychological forces rather than psychic ones or the much-discredited animal magnetism. The actual practice of hypnosis, as mentioned in Chapter 2, dates back to antiquity, when it was called 'temple sleep' by the Babylonians, Egyptians, and Greeks, and used in religious-magical rituals.

After psychiatry made the practice somewhat respectable, Mesmer received some reluctant, posthumous, and unwarranted praise as its founder. His real discovery (or rediscovery) of the healing energy, animal magnetism, continues to be regarded as a myth.

Baron Karl von Reichenbach, a German scientist born in 1788, did not hold much esteem for Mesmer's 'phantasmagoria,' which was the Baron's word for lavender gowns, wands, bacquets, and general showmanship. However, he did believe in the theory of animal magnetism. And he spent the last 30 years of his life trying to prove it.

The Odic Force

Considered one of the most distinguished scientists of the 19th century, Reichenbach was the discoverer of kerosene, as well as a highly respected metallurgist, chemist, technologist, and meteorologist. It was therefore a shock to the world of establishment science when a man of such eminence suddenly announced his discovery of a healing energy, which he called Od, or the Odic force. Reichenbach found the term more apt than animal magnetism since the name Od comes from the Norse god, Odin, and signifies great power.

Reichenbach was convinced that Od was a force that permeated all of nature. And to prove its existence, he conducted hundreds of experiments for nearly three decades. The experiments, he said, demonstrated that certain sensitive people could observe emanations from crystals and magnets; they could also, he added, see auras around human beings.

The Odic force, according to Reichenbach, was to be found in magnets, crystals, the human body, the sun, the moon, the stars, heat, electricity, friction, chemical action, and the whole material universe.

He analyzed the positive and negative polar effects of Od, and demonstrated how liquids and solids could be charged with it.

His findings were best summarized by Westlake in *The Pattern of Health* (The word 'odyle' was used interchangeably with Od.):

1. Odyle is a universal property of matter in variable and unequal distribution both in space and time.

2. It interpenetrates and fills the structure of the universe. It cannot be eliminated or isolated from anything in nature.

3. It quickly penetrates and courses through everything.

4. It flows in concentrated form from special sources such as heat, friction, sound, electricity, light, the moon, solar and stellar rays, chemical action, organic vital activity of plants and animals, especially man.

5. It possesses polarity. There is both negative odyle, which gives a sensation of coolness and is pleasant; and positive odyle, which gives a sensation of warmth and discomfort.

6. It can be conducted, metals, glass, resin, silk, and water all being perfect conductors.

7. It is radiated to a distance, and these rays penetrate through clothes, bedclothes, boards, and walls.

8. Substances can be charged with odyle, or odyle may be transferred from one body to another. This is effected by contact and requires a certain amount of time.

9. It is luminous, either as a luminous glow or as a flame, showing blue at the negative and yellow-red at the positive. These flames can be made to flow in any direction.

10. Human beings are odyle containers, with polarity, and are luminous over the whole surface; hence the so-called aura surrounding the physical body. In the 24 hours a periodic fluctuation, a decrease and increase of odylic power, occurs in the human body.

Scientific Precision

Unlike Mesmer, Reichenbach conducted his experiments with the same scientific precision that had earned him such renown in other areas. He realized that he was dealing with a mysterious and elusive power in an area that was considered occult, but his love of truth kept him on the quest.

Reichenbach was convinced that Od could explain the link between science and the supernatural. Because the force could move objects without conscious effort, it shed light on many psychic phenomena; it even validated the occasional ghost or 'corpse-light' seen over a new grave.

Reichenbach's theories, alas, were given scarcely more credibility than Mesmer's. All of the conclusions drawn from his careful, scientific experiments were, according to orthodoxy, due to the imagination of his sensitive subjects. His experiments were termed fables, and his entire work in the field was called "one of the most deplorable aberrations that has for a long time affected a human brain."

But Reichenbach responded to his critics with a good deal of intelligent spunk: " ... ever since science has existed, ignorance has assumed the right of judging and condemning that which it could not understand ... He who assumes the right publicly to sit in judgment, and to pronounce sentence on a scientific work, is, before all things, bound in duty to inform himself thoroughly of its contents; and he is further bound to support his sentence, as all public judges do, by the reasons on which he thinks himself justified in pronouncing it."

Readers interested in studying this man's experiments and his defence of them should read William Gregory's translation of Reichenbach's *Researches on Magnetism, Electricity, Heat, Light, Crystallization, and Chemical Attraction in Relation to the Vital Force,* and Reichenbach's *The Mysterious Odic Force,* the latter available from Aquarian Press, Denington Estate, Wellingborough, Northants, NN8 2RQ.

Discredited, ridiculed, his writings suppressed, Reichenbach survived such disgrace for 25 years and died at the age of 80. Gustav

Fechner, his friend and fellow scientist, said: "Up to the last days of his life, he grieved at the thought of having to die without obtaining recognition for his system, and such was the tragic fate that actually befell him."

Although the healing energy gained no scientific acceptance during the 19th century, the psychic aspects of Mesmer's animal magnetism became widespread. Throughout Europe, certain magnetized or mesmerized individuals continued to fall into trance and become clairvoyant; they saw auras and happenings at long distance; and some prescribed medicines.

Spiritualism and Christian Science

Mesmerism was introduced to the United States by a French magnetist named Charles Poyen in 1838. It was his lectures that were largely responsible for the rise of two movements in the United States that continue to flourish: (1) spiritualism, in its first self-conscious organized form, and (2) Christian Science.

Communication with spirits has been described to us since the beginning of history. And although the medieval church accepted the reality of such phenomena, those engaged in such communications were persecuted. Such actions continued to be heavily frowned upon until mesmerism opened the door.

In 1848, two girls known as the Fox sisters heard strange knockings on their walls in Hydesville, N.Y. They spoke to the spirit producing the noises, arranged a code, and began to receive messages.* This event created a sensation and achieved unusual credibility – primarily because the way had been paved a few years earlier by a young prophet named Andrew Jackson Davis.

Davis was 17 when he became acquainted with mesmerism and found himself to be clairvoyant. After communicating with spirits, he diagnosed diseases and prescribed cures that apparently worked. After his psychic sense had fully developed, he wrote a book, which he said was divinely revealed. The name of the book was *The Principles of Nature, Her Divine Revelations*. Because Davis's authenticity as a medium and prophet were vouched for by a group of respected doctors, ministers, and editors, the work received wide acclaim. It opens as follows:

---

* The messages reportedly revealed that the sender was one Charles Rosna, a door-to-door peddler who had years before been robbed and murdered on the premises, then buried in the cellar.

Liquid Fire

"In the beginning the Univercoelum was one boundless, undefinable and unimaginable ocean of liquid fire! The most vigorous and ambitious imagination is not capable of forming an adequate conception of the height and depth and length and breadth thereof. There was one vast expanse of liquid substance. It was without bounds – inconceivable – and with qualities and essences incomprehensible.

"This was the original condition of matter. It was without forms, for it was but one form. It had not set motions, but it was an eternity of motion. It was without parts, for it was a whole. Particles did not exist, but the whole was as one particle. There were not suns, but it was one eternal sun.

"It had no beginning, and it was without end. It had not length, for it was a vortex of one eternity. It had not circles, for it was one infinite circle. It had not disconnected power, but it was the very essence of all power. Its inconceivable magnitude and constitution were such as not to develop forces, but omnipotent power.

"Matter and power were existing as a whole, inseparable. The matter contained the substance to produce all suns, all worlds, and systems of worlds, throughout the immensity of space. It contained the original and essential principle that is displayed throughout the immensity of space, controlling worlds and systems of worlds, and producing motion, life, sensation, and intelligence, to be impartially disseminated upon their surfaces as ultimates."

This primeval fire, said Davis, gradually became condensed through a process of evolution into an ordered universe of solar system. The goal of this process, he added, is "the individualization of Spirit, the production of man, the ultimate, to the end that communion and sympathy may be established between the creator and the created."

In another work, *The Physician*, he writes: "Disease is a want of equilibrium in the circulation of the spiritual principle through the physical organization. In plainer language, disease is a discord, and the discord must exist primarily in the spiritual forces by which the organism is actuated and governed."

The revelations and prophecies of Davis stimulated and 'spiritized' a large section of the population. The atmosphere thus created was unusually receptive for the experiences of the Fox sisters. As a result, many people organized mediumistic groups, which eventually became spiritualist churches.

Phineas Parkhurst Quimby of Lebanon, N.H. (previously mentioned in Chapter 2) was 36 years old when he heard the French magnetist, Charles Poyen, lecture on mesmerism in 1838. Fascinated, he became a professional mesmerist himself. And after locating a suitable clairvoyant, he rapidly learned how to cultivate the trance state towards the diagnosis and healing of diseases.

After a while, Quimby came to the conclusion that the clairvoyant's diagnoses were due not to spirits but to thought-reading. In other words, the clairvoyant was simply reproducing the decision that the patient had already arrived at concerning his condition. If this were true, then there should be no need of a clairvoyant. The patient, in the right state of mind, should be able to cure himself. All illness, he decided, was basically a matter of the mind; disease resulted from mistaken beliefs. The cure, therefore, must rest in changing the patient's negative convictions.

Acting upon his theory, Quimby developed an inordinately successful method of healing based on *rapport*, suggestion, and an unknown energy.

According to Frank Podmore's *From Mesmerism to Christian Science,* the local papers in Maine, where Quimby lived, contained many descriptions of his methods. The following from the *Bangor Jeffersonian* is especially interesting: "He says the mind is what it thinks it is, and that if it contends against the thought of disease and creates for itself an ideal form of health, that form impresses itself upon the animal spirit and through that upon the body."

The system defined above is very similar to the 'magic' of the ancient *kahunas*, who were discussed in Chapter 2.

Quimby's patients, when questioned, spoke of the vitality that accompanied his words and how they felt 'recharged' in his presence. Quimby found that once a *rapport* had been established between himself and a patient, even absent healing could be accomplished.

Mary Baker Eddy

One of Quimby's patients was Mary Baker Eddy. She was very impressed with his healing methods and reportedly studied them. After his death, Mrs Eddy discovered that when she became ill, she was able to heal herself without Quimby's aid. After developing her own techniques, she instituted the doctrine of Christian Science. Although she always claimed to be the organization's sole founder, many of Quimby's disciples believed her ideas to be based upon his.

One tenet of Mrs Eddy's was her belief in "malicious animal magnetism": Since mental healers can effect their cures at long distance by means of a certain energy, it stands to reason that they can effect misfortune through the same process. Mrs Eddy was said to be terrified by the possibility of receiving malign thought waves from her enemies, and modern Christian Scientists continue the study of methods to avoid malicious animal magnetism.

While mesmerism and animal magnetism were absorbed into spirtualism and mental healing in the U.S., they were taking a different direction in France. Until the latter part of the 19th century, all research on animal magnetism had been condemned by the French Académie des Sciences in Paris, and hypnosis was considered a disreputable practice.

But when an eminent doctor named Jean-Martin Charcot presented his views "on diverse nervous states determined by the hypnotization of hysterics," the Académie felt his work was unrelated to animal magnetism and accepted his findings. Hypnosis had become acceptable!

This news provoked a veritable avalanche of doctors eager to investigate the phenomenon, and they poured into Paris from all over the world in order to witness Charcot's demonstrations. Among those attending his lectures on hypnosis was Sigmund Freud. And it is very doubtful that without hypnosis the father of psychoanalysis would have ever developed his famous theory.

Like Quimby, Freud used hypnosis as a launching pad for new techniques – free association, for example. Both Quimby and Freud arrived independently at the conclusion that the *rapport* between analyst and patient was essential.

Edgar Cayce

Without the phenomenon of mesmerism, the United States might never have recognized the healing abilities of its most famous psychic, Edgar Cayce. For although he exhibited his psychic development as a child, his clairvoyant ability to make medical diagnoses was manifested only after he'd experienced hypnosis.

Cayce diagnosed patients clairvoyantly for 43 years, and his accuracy, as well as his integrity, have remained largely undisputed. When he died in 1945, he left 14,000 documented stenographic records of the telepathic-clairvoyant statements he had given for more than 6,000 people. These 'readings' are now on file in the library of the

Association for Research and Enlightenment, Inc., a psychical research society that continues to preserve and investigate Cayce's findings in Virginia Beach, Va.

While in the trance state, Cayce seemed able to 'tune in' telepathically on an individual's mind and body; most of his diagnoses were made at long distance, for all he required was the patient's name and address.

After a group of Kentucky physicians employed Cayce's gifts to diagnose their own patients, his fame spread. On October 9, 1910, *The New York Times* carried a two-page feature on him, thus adding to his renown and inspiring people from all over the nation to seek his advice.

Cayce's prescriptions included diet, spinal adjustments, medicines, and vibratory treatments. In other words, he treated the body physically, biochemically, and dynamically. His approach was holistic in that he believed health to be dependent upon the proper relationship and balance of body-mind-spirit.

"The human body," said Cayce in one of his readings, "is made up of electronic vibrations, with each atom and element of the body, each organ and organism having its electronic unit of vibration necessary for the sustenance of, and equilibrium in, that particular organism. Each unit, then, being a cell or a unit of life in itself has its capacity of reproducing itself by the first law as is known of reproduction-division.

"When a force in any organ, or element of the body, becomes deficient in its ability to reproduce that equilibrium necessary for the sustenance of the physical existence and its reproduction, that portion becomes deficient in electronic energy. This may come from internal forces through lack of eliminations produced in the system, or by the lack of other agencies to meet its requirements in the body."

The Wet Cell

The above, which appeared in Thomas Sugrue's classic book about Cayce, *There Is a River*, was an explanation for the clairvoyant's prescribed use of certain appliances of an electrical nature. The device known as the wet cell, for instance, operated on the premise that a very low electrical charge set up in a wet solution of acid, metal, and copper sulphate can be unleashed through solutions of gold chloride, camphor, or iodine; the vibratory impulse can be transferred to the body, causing it to extract more of the particular property in the solution from its digested foods.

Cayce's readings imply that he perceived man's organs, systems, and cells to be composed of units of energy that possessed their own individual awareness. Like other psychics, he described a flow of energy in the body, that is shaped like the figure eight, with the lines crossing at the solar plexus. (The solar plexus, one recalls, is also the site of the *kahunas'* low self.) There is much evidence to support the view that many of Cayce's prescriptions worked on the individual's second, or etheric, body.

Cayce the man, Cayce the healer, and Cayce the prophet are all such remarkable phenomena that it is impossible to condense them here. Everyone who has not yet done so should read the many books that have been written about Edgar Cayce and his teachings.

A progression of thought now comes into view:

(1) Mesmer, strongly influenced by the energy theories of Pythagoras and Paracelsus (the *pneuma* and *archaeus*) encounters this force on his own and calls it animal magnetism.

(2) Von Reichenbach, one of the few scientists who did not disdain Mesmer's findings, comes upon the same power. He calls it the Odic force and tries to establish its existence scientifically.

(3) Disciples of Mesmer note that persons experiencing contact with animal magnetism exhibit an unusual state of mind. This is referred to first as mesmerism, later as hypnosis.

(4) Hypnosis leads to the mental healing of Quimby, Davis, Cayce, and even Christian Science; it also leads to Freud's theory of the unconscious.

In spite of certain divergencies, this sequence of events should allow one to perceive a certain pattern of consistency or thread of reason — not obvious, to be sure, but visible. The mystery, however, is far from solved. The truth of the matter, or, better, the truth of the energy seems to lie within a knotty skein that first entices and then eludes unravelment.

6

HAHNEMANN AND HOMOEOPATHY

Samuel Hahnemann (1755-1843) was one of the medical history's epochal figures. Known as the founder of homoeopathy, Hahnemann recognized a healing energy that he referred to sometimes as the vital force and sometimes as the dynamis. When this energy is disturbed, he said, there occurs a deviation from natural health that results in the symptoms of illness. In order to restore this vital force, which could be blocked by an imbalance of body, mind, or spirit, Hahnemann advocated remedies prepared from natural sources such as plants, minerals, and animals. When the vital force was returned to its natural equilibrium, he believed, the health of the individual was also renewed.

In Hahnemann's own words: "In the healthy condition of man, the spiritual vital force (autocracy), the dynamis that animates the material body (organism), rules with unbounded sway, and retains all the parts of the organism in admirable, harmonious, vital operation, as regards both sensations and functions, so that our indwelling reason-gifted mind can freely employ this living, healthy instrument for the higher purposes of our existence."

The above, from Hahnemann's *Organon of Medicine*, suggests that he, like so many other holistic healers, from Pythagoras on, may have believed the body to be, primarily, a vehicle for the soul.

The Law of Similars
Homoeopathic remedies are based on the law of similars – like cures like. The medicines consist of tiny doses of a substance that in healthy persons causes symptoms resembling those of the disease being treated. Quinine, for example, which is used to cure malaria, produces in healthy persons the symptoms of malaria.

This theory is an old one. Hippocrates said: "Through the like, disease is produced, and through the application of the like, it is cured." And Paracelsus said that if given in small doses, what makes a man ill also cures him.

The law of similars was also referred to in principle by Nicander and Xenocrates of the Greek schools; Varro, Quintus Serenus, Celsus, and Galen of the Roman schools; Basil Valentine, a Benedictine monk, and others. But it was conceived by Hahnemann to be the general law of medical action and first advanced by him as an actual system of therapy.

In trying to explain homoeopathy, Sir John Weir, dean of British homoeopathic physicians and personal physician of the Queen and Royal Family, recently said: "Remember, it is the patient who has to cure himself; the drug cannot cure him; the drug is only the stimulus which starts the vital reaction."

And the vital reaction re-establishes the physiological equilibrium.

"In order to bring this about," explains William Gutman, M.D., president of the Foundation for Homoeopathic Research, Inc., "a drug is chosen which is known to have a similar effect upon the bio-chemistry and the cells of the body as the disease-provoking agent. Given in sufficiently small doses, this drug will act as stimulus and remedy to provoke a stronger reaction from the defence mechanisms of the body, which automatically restore the physiological balance."

Although homoeopathic remedies are roughly analagous to vaccinations and allergy shots, where toxins are introduced into the body in order to immunize it, there is a great difference. First, homoeopaths do not believe in injections; second, they do not believe that only the disease-making substance must be given. What they do believe is that *anything* (mineral, animal, vegetable) that causes a certain group of symptoms in a healthy person will cure the same symptoms in an ill person. Homoeopathic doses, also, are much, much smaller than those used in vaccines; and they are prescribed to treat the whole person – body, mind, and soul.

In an address to physicians called *Modern Medicine and Homoeopathy,* Dr Gutman states that homoeopathy anticipated the principle of antiallergic treatment on a very broad basis that encompassed all pathological conditions. The word al-lergy, he adds, actually means altered energy.* And it is this alteration of physical

* From the Greek words: *allos*, meaning different or other; and *ergia*, meaning work.

energies that is the basic cause of every disease; the alteration is accompanied by a highly increased sensitivity of the diseased cell to the disease-producing agent, as well as to the curative drug.

"Homoeopathy," Dr Gutman continues, "has applied this broader concept of allergy to a treatment of every pathological condition, by giving small doses of a drug which is able to produce a similar condition.

"Most pathological conditions can be reproduced by some substance. The classic example, because it was mentioned already by Hippocrates, is hemorrhagic cystitis which, as he stated, can be produced by cantharis, but also cured by it."

Born in Meissen, Germany, Hahnemann studied medicine in Leipzig, Vienna, and Erlangen. Practising in Leipzig after his graduation, the young doctor grew to loathe the medicine of his time, which included bloodletting with the use of leeches and cups, violent purges, *ad nauseam*. He was determined to find alternatives.

Always fascinated by the principle of 'like cures like', referred to by so many physicians before him, Hahnemann wondered if the proposition could be proved. He reasoned that if there were credibility in the idea that diseases are cured by medicines that have the power to provoke similar symptoms, there would be only one way to determine it scientifically. This would be to give a medicine to a healthy person and observe the effects, since a healthy person would be the only kind of person in whom a symptom similar to the particular disease could be excited.

This would give a scientific basis for a comparison between symptoms of drugs and the symptoms of disease.

Experiment with Cinchona (Quinine)

While translating a book of Scottish remedies by Cullen into German, Hahnemann read that cinchona (quinine) was highly recommended as a cure for chills and fever. He began to experiment with the drug upon himself and found that it did indeed cause chills and fever. He then searched medical literature for records of illnesses, poisonings, accidental cures, etc., as a basis for further experimentation and corroboration. Enlisting the aid of a few colleagues, he continued to experiment upon healthy persons, carefully observing and recording.

After several years of this work, he compiled a collection of drug phenomena so comprehensive that he believed he could scientifically formulate the law of similars. Under this law, cinchona (quinine) cures malaria not because it destroys toxins, but because it produces the same symptoms. Like cures like.

For the next 50 years, Hahnemann determined what remedies produced what symptoms by experimenting on himself and colleagues with about 99 drugs. His observations of their effects upon the human body are considered by many to be among the most accurate and extensive investigations ever made by any single observer throughout the annals of medical history.

After the first 16 years of research and 'provings' (the homoeopathic term for testing drugs on healthy individuals), Hahnemann had compiled an extensive listing and description of remedies, which was known as his *materia medica.* And in 1810, he published his *Organon of Medicine,* postulating his medical theories.

Hahnemann's *Organon* and his system of homoeopathy so incensed the medical profession that he was dismissed from his position as lecturer at the University of Leipzig and forced to give up his practice. It was fortunate that Ferdinand, the Duke of Anhalt Kothen in France, invited him to be court physician. For it was here that Hahnemann's principles gained wide acceptance.

Theory of Potentization
Many people believe that Hahnemann's crowning achievement was not so much his law of similars but his theory of potentization and the infinitesimal dose.

Disturbed about the side effects from conventional drugs, Hahnemann began to dilute his remedies in order to make them safe. In the process, he discovered that the weaker doses appeared to be the most potent. By reducing the density of the mass, he was apparently setting free powers that were previously latent.

Struck by the idea of releasing latent powers through dilution with alcohol and water, he changed the word, dilution, to potentization. Homoeopathic potentization may be described as a physical process — through dilution and the mechanical agitation known as succussion — by which the dynamic energy latent in crude substances is liberated, developed, and modified for use as medicines.

Potentization is achieved by placing one drop of the actual healing substance into 99 drops of solvent. After this is shaken, another drop is taken and mixed with another 99 drops of solvent; this is also shaken. The process is duplicated five times, ten times, *ad infinitum.*

And the number of times is indicated by the figure 5X or 10X on the remedy's label.

The extraordinary thing is that the more diluted the medicine, the more potent it becomes. And more remarkable still is the fact that after the 30th dilution, absolutely none of the original substance remains. Yet there are labels marked 100X and even 1,000,000X! Hahnemann believed that it was the energy of the substance, rather than the substance itself, which healed. In his own words from the *Organon,* he gets to the heart of the matter – or, rather, the heart of the energy:

"It is not in the corporeal atoms of these highly dynamized medicines, nor their physical or mathematical surfaces (with which the higher energies of the dynamized medicines are being interpreted but vainly as still sufficiently material) that the medicinal energy is found. More likely, there lies invisible in the moistened globule or in its solution, an unveiled, liberated, specific, medicinal force contained in the medicinal substance which acts dynamically by contact with the living animal fibre upon the whole organism (without communicating to it anything material however highly attenuated) and acts more strongly the more free and more immaterial the energy has become through the dynamization.

"Is it then so utterly impossible for our age, celebrated for its wealth in clear thinkers, to think of dynamic energy as something non-corporeal, since we see daily phenomena which cannot be explained in any other manner? If one looks upon something nauseous and becomes inclined to vomit, did a material emetic come into his stomach which compels him to this anti-peristaltic movement? Was it not solely the dynamic effect of the nauseating aspect upon his imagination? And if one raises his arm, does it occur through a material visible instrument? A lever? Is it not solely the conceptual dynamic energy of his will which raises it?"

According to Edward F. Kingkinger, in an article called 'Metaphysical Science in Homoeopathy,' which appeared in the *Homoeopathic Digest,* Vol. 3, questions concerning potentization and the infinitesimal dose have caused much discord among homoeopaths. The subject has, in fact, he said, divided them into two distinct groups known as the materialists and the dynamists.

Kingkinger also points out that the discovery of the atom bomb fully verified Hahnemann's theory of potentization and the infinitesimal dose. The atom bomb, he explains, is a tragic triumph for the homoeopathic law of similars. The weapon's chief ingredient is uranium nitricum, which is a great remedy for diseases such as diabetes, degeneration of the liver, high blood-pressure, and dropsy — all illnesses that are caused by it, as we have learned from the Japanese about after-effects of the bomb.

Nature's 'Minimum Principle'

Dr Gutman states that the use of the smallest dosage in homoeopathy is based upon a general principle of natural science, derived from physics, the so-called minimum principle of Maupertuis and Euler,* according to which a tendency exists in nature to achieve the greatest possible effect through the smallest possible means.

"From the application of the 'Law of Similars,' it follows logically that the dosis of a drug must be much smaller than the usual physiological dosis, as is the case in the similar anti-allergic treatment. The small homoeopathic dose surpasses in smallness such doses (as in anti-allergic treatment) and, at the same time, increases its energy of action. This is due to the pharmacological process of so-called potentization of the drug, a process invented by Hahnemann.

"Through a series of successions (shakings), or triturations (pulverizations) with physiologically more inert substances such as milk sugar and diluted alcohol, the drug substance is brought into a state of ever greater dispersion, which increases the surface and thus the surface energy on which all drug-cell interaction depends. To give an example, a substance compared in its mass to a cube of 1 cm^3 can be transformed through a process of trituration as applied in the process of potentization in Homoeopathy to a state where its surface, according to length of time of trituration, grows to 60-600 m^2. The process of potentization of the drug used in Homoeopathy thus increases the surface enormously.

"The greater the degree of potentization, the greater the surface and with it the surface energy on which depend increasing absorption, diffusion, speed of chemical reaction, electric potential and catalytic actions. These are the principal means through which all drug action takes place, an action that consists of altering the function of the cell membranes and influencing the cellular enzymes through surface action. The homoeopathic preparation of drugs completely fulfils this

* Eighteenth-century Swiss mathematicians.

requirement by bringing the drug into a physical state which increases its ability to act; at the same time, because of the small physical amount needed, such preparation abolishes any untoward side effect.

"The homoeopathic dose in its lower potencies equals in amount, but also in its physical state, the catalysts and enzymes of the body on which all body processes ultimately depend and through which also the drug actions are effectuated."

According to Stuart Close, M.D., in his book *The Genius of Homoeopathy*, the discovery of the law of similars did not create homoeopathy. Many, he writes, before Hahnemann, from Hippocrates down, had glimpses of the law, and some had tried to make use of it therapeutically; but all failed because of their inability to properly graduate and adapt the dose.

The law of similars, then, was of no practical use until the related principle of potentization and the minimum dose was discovered; "and that was not until Hahnemann, anticipating by 100 years the modern conceptions of matter and force, hit upon the mathematico-mechanical expedient of preparing the drug by *dilution according to scale in a definite proportion of drug to inert vehicle.*" If that discovery had not been made, Hahnemann would have progressed no further than Hippocrates.

Originally, homoeopathic solutions were prepared manually, using mortar and pestle plus glass vial. The handmade potencies are still preferred by many, but most homoeopathic pharmacists use machines.

Dr Close also more fully explains the difference between homoeopathic remedies and vaccines, serums, allergy shots, etc., helping to clarify a distinction that many people find difficult to grasp.

The basic idea of serums and vaccines is to so modify a virulent animal virus, toxin, or other pathological product that it may be used safely for therapeutic purposes. In this sense, it is not unlike homoeopathic potentization.

But, writes Dr Close: "Considered as a technical process such a method is highly objectionable because it involves so many uncertainties. The living organism is an infinitely complex thing, when we consider the almost innumerable mechanical, chemical and vital processes going on within its constantly changing fluids and solids.

"Many of these processes are very imperfectly understood. There are no means of accurately registering and measuring all these activities; no means of determining exactly what these changes are; nor how they are modified by the introduction of the foreign morbid substance used.

"In comparing this method with the Hahnemann process it is only necessary to point out:

"1. The Hahnemannian process is purely physical, objective and mechanical.

"2. It does not involve any uncertain, unseen, unreliable nor unmeasurable factor. Its elements are simply the substance or drug to be potentiated, a vehicle consisting of sugar of milk, alcohol, or water, in certain quantities and definite proportions; manipulation under conditions which are entirely under control and so simple that a child could comply with them.

"3. The resulting product is stable, or may easily be made so; in fact it is almost indestructible; and the experience of a century in its use under homoeopathic methods and principles has proved it to be efficient and reliable in the treatment of all forms of disease amenable to medication.

"4. The process is practically illimitable. Potentization of medicine by this method may be carried to any extent desired or required."

Barbarous Medical Practices

As mentioned earlier, the medical situation in Hahnemann's day was in a very sorry state. Ideas that now seem barbarous were common practice, and they often held tragic consequences.

In France, for example, in the hospitals of Paris during just one year more than six million leeches were used and more than 200,000 pounds of blood was spilled. And poor King Louis XIII, also in the period of a year, was given 47 bleedings, 215 emetics or purgatives, and 312 enemas. (His physician, a Dr Bouvard, was considered one of the best.) The mortality rate from such practices was, as one might expect, rather high.*

In the U.S., the death of George Washington on December 14, 1799, may well have been contributed to by the heavy, continuous bleedings to which he was subjected; for at the time of his death, he was reported to be almost completely exsanguinated.** Small wonder

---

* Stuart Close, *The Genius of Homoeopathy, Lectures and Essays on Homoeopathic Philosophy* (Calcutta: Haren & Brother, 1967), p. 29.
** *Ibid.*

that his deathbed request to those in attendance was: "I thank you for your attentions; but I pray you to take no more trouble about me. Let me go off quietly ..."

Hahnemann's Attitude to Allopaths

It was in this atmosphere of medical chaos that Hahnemann, shortly before he died, wrote a new introduction to the sixth edition of his *Organon*, in which his attitude toward allopaths is apparent:

"It seems that the unhallowed principal business of the old school of medicine (allopathy) is to render incurable if not fatal the majority of diseases, those made chronic through ignorance by continually weakening and tormenting the already debilitated patient by the further addition of new destructive drug diseases. When this pernicious practice has become a habit and one is rendered insensible to the admonitions of conscience, this becomes a very easy business indeed ...

"This non-healing art, which for many centuries has been firmly established in full possession of the power to dispose of the life and death of patients according to its own good will and pleasure, and in that period has shortened the lives of ten times as many human beings as the most destructive wars, and rendered many millions of patients more diseased and wretched than they were originally – this allopathy, I have, in the introduction to the former editions of this book, considered more in detail. Now I shall consider only its exact opposite, the true healing art, discovered by me and now somewhat more perfected. Examples are given to prove that striking cures performed in former times were always due to remedies basically homoeopathic and found by the physician accidentally and contrary to the then prevailing methods of therapeutics.

"As regards the latter (homoeopathy) it is quite otherwise. It can easily convince very [sic] reflecting person that the diseases of man are not caused by any substances, any acridity, that is to say, any disease-matter, but that they are solely spirit-like (dynamic) derangements of the spirit-like power (the vital principle) that animates the human body.

"Homoeopathy knows that a cure can only take place by the reaction of the vital force against the rightly chosen remedy that has been ingested, and that the cure will be certain and rapid in proportion to the strength with which the vital force still prevails in the patient.

"Hence homoeopathy *avoids everything in the slightest degree enfeeble*,* and as much as possible every excitation of pain, for pain also diminishes the strength and hence it employs for the cure ONLY those medicines whose power for altering and deranging (dynamically) the health it knows *accurately*, and from these it selects one whose pathogenetic power (its medicinal disease) is capable of removing the natural disease in question by similarity (*similia similibus*), and thus it administers to the patient in simple form, but in rare and minute doses so small that, without occasioning pain or weakening, they just suffice to remove the natural malady whence this result: that without weakening, injuring or torturing him in the very least, the natural disease is extinguished, and the patient, even whilst he is getting better, gains in strength and thus is cured – an apparently easy but actually troublesome and difficult business, and one requiring much thought, but which restores the patient without suffering in a short time to perfect health – and thus it is a salutary and blessed business.

"Thus homoeopathy is a perfectly simple system of medicine, remaining always fixed in its principles as in its practice, which, like the doctrine whereon it is based, if rightly apprehended will be found to be complete (and therefore serviceable). What is clearly pure in doctrine and practice should be self-evident, and all backward sliding to the pernicious routinism of the old school that is as much its antithesis as night is to day should cease to vaunt itself with the honourable name of Homoeopathy.

SAMUEL HAHNEMANN"

"Kothen, March 28, 1833
Confirmed Paris, 4 184 –**"

Homoeopathy was introduced to the U.S. in 1820 when Dr Constantine Hering, known as the American father of homoeopathy, founded the Hahnemann Medical College, which still exists in

---

* "Homoeopathy sheds not a drop of blood, administers no emetics, purgatives, laxatives, or diaphoretics, drives off no external affection by external means, prescribes no hot or unknown mineral baths or medicated clysters, applies no Spanish flies or mustard plasters, no setons, no issues, excites no ptyalism, burns not with moxa or red-hot iron to the very bone, and so forth, but gives with its own hand its own preparations of simple uncompounded medicines, which it is accurately acquainted with, never subdues pain by opium, etc."

** "Hahnemann did not put in his manuscript the exact date, leaving this probably until the book would go to the printer, but Dr Haehl suggests February 1842 as the date, according to a manuscript copy made by Madame Hahnemann. William Boericke (translator)."

Philadelphia. The American Institute of Homoeopathy was formed in 1844, two years before the American Medical Association (A.M.A.)

The homoeopaths, then, constitute the oldest medical group in the nation. The system seemed to be growing in popularity for a while, and during a yellow-fever epidemic in New Orleans in 1853, homoeopathy was reported by many to have been more effective than allopathy.

In 1900, when there were about 22 homoeopathic colleges in the U.S., the practice began to die out due to pressure from the A.M.A.

But, according to many homoeopathists, their system is making a comeback, is, in fact, advancing. This is due to modern healing concepts that support the theory, as well as to growing disillusionment with today's drugs and their harmful side effects. Homoeopathic remedies, as we have learned, are absolutely safe.

In England, the Royal Family has used homoeopathic doctors for three generations. Great Britain, through an act of Parliament, has safeguarded the teaching and practice of homoeopathy within the National Health scheme. It is also well-known in Russia, France, Germany, South America, and India.

A few well-known personalities who chose homoeopathic treatment on the basis of personal experience were John D. Rockefeller, Sr., Henry Ford, Sr., Kettering, and Pope Pius XII.

Epilepsy Cured by Homoeopathy

According to Dr Gutman, homoeopathy often succeeds where other treatment fails, and it proves curative in severe conditions where medicine otherwise can only palliate. As an example, he described a 40-year-old woman who had suffered 20 years from epilepsy. After a homoeopathic treatment with high potencies of argentum nitricum, one of a number of drugs capable of producing in its toxic effects epileptic convulsions, and chosen from them because of its closest similarity with the attacks and general constitutional reactions of the patient, the attacks gradually disappeared.

"Without any further treatment," said Dr Gutman, "the former patient, for two years, has now been free of any attacks. There are similar cases of complete cure on record, and also cases in many other fields of pathology, not amenable to usual drug treatment, except palliation."

In the field of infectious diseases, he adds, the homoeopathic drug is not aimed at the germ and its destruction, but at the host, establishing resistance on the immunological and cell level, thus overcoming the infection. Experiments have shown that the homoeopathic drug is able to act as an antigen, in addition to having a specific stimulating effect on the cells of the diseased organ.

Dr Gutman continued: "Homoeopathic drug treatment is, therefore, independent of drug resistance of germs, a growing problem, and applicable and successful in many cases where antibiotics and chemotherapeutic drugs fail, or are not tolerated. It has proved curative also in the field of virus infections which are not susceptible to antibiotics, as the problem of influenza and colds shows. There are 70–100 different strains of cold viruses and a number of influenza viruses known with ever-changing antigenic patterns. Homoeopathy deals easily with these conditions, since its vast materia medica meets the problem of the host resistance level and through a multiplicity of drugs with antigenic effect from which the indicated drug can be chosen according to the different symptomatology produced by different strains."

Potent Dosage of Pulsatilla

My own experience with homoeopathy has been highly rewarding. I was given a remedy for hay fever, and it worked. Knowing that the homoeopathic doctor analyzes his patients psychically as well as physically and chooses his remedies accordingly, I was curious to find out what had been given me. And although he was reluctant to do so, believing such disclosures unprofessional, the doctor finally informed me that I'd been given a potent dosage of pulsatilla. Fortunately, I had a copy of Kent's *Homoeopathic Materia Medica* (a list and discussion of remedies) in my home, so I looked it up.

Before quoting the description of pulsatilla, I should emphasize that the homoeopathic doctor studies the whole person and prescribes a remedy that not only duplicates the symptoms of his physical illness but that of his personality frailties as well. And although I was not particularly flattered by the following account, the medicine, did, after all, work.

Pulsatilla, as described in the *Materia Medica*, "is said to be a very good medicine *for women*, for blondes, especially for *tearful blondes*. It is one of the polycrests and one of the medicines most frequently used, as well as often abused.

"The pulsatilla patient is an interesting one, found in any household where there are plenty of young girls. She is tearful, plethoric, and generally has little credit for being sick from her appearances; yet she is most nervous, fidgety, changeable, easily led and easily persuaded. While she is mild, gentle, and tearful, yet she is remarkably irritable, not in the sense of pugnacity, but easily irritated, extremely touchy, always feels slighted or fears she will be slighted, sensible to every social influence. Melancholia, sadness, weeping, despair, religious despair, fanatical; full of notions and whims; imaginative; extremely excitable. She imagines the company of the opposite sex a dangerous thing to cultivate, and that it is dangerous to do certain things well established in society as good for the human race ...

"With such a mental state the general state of the body is worse in a warm room and relieved by motion ...

"Many symptoms worse [sic] after eating. It is often only a lump in the stomach, but the mental and nervous symptoms also are worse after eating ...

"In pulsatilla patients the skin feels feverish and hot, while the temperature of the body is normal. There is aggravation from [too] much clothing; she wants to wear a thin dress even in moderately cold weather ...

"Pulsatilla is very useful in hay fever. The management of hay fever requires considerable study because you have to deal with the troublesome imaginations of the patient, he will refuse to let you study him ... "

Although I'm not sure that the pulsatilla fits me exactly (for one thing, I'm not a blonde), certainly I was grateful that the remedy known as lachesis had not been prescribed. Lachesis is a genus of viper, and the homoeopathic medicine (in a refined, potentized state) is extracted from its venom.

The Lachesis Personality

As one can imagine, the lachesis personality is an extremely nasty one, and, oddly enough, most often male.

Kent's *Materia Medica* says that lachesis is a frequently indicated remedy and one that requires much study before use. Lachesis seems to fit a large section of the human race, "for the race is pretty well filled up with snake as to disposition and character, and this venom only causes to appear that which (already) is in man ...

"Nothing stands out more boldly than the self-consciousness, the self-conceit, the envy, the hatred, the revenge and the cruelty of the man. These things, of course, are matters of self-consciousness, an improper love of self. Confusion of the mind to insanity. All sorts of impulsive insanity. The mind is tired. The patient puts on an appearance like the maudling of a drunkard, talks with thick lips and thick tongue, blunders and stumbles, only partly finishing words; the face is purple and the head is hot ... Unwarranted jealousy and suspicion."

Some of the women for whom lachesis is prescribed, according to Kent, sound somewhat schizophrenic, and one wonders if the remedy has ever been used for that purpose. This type of woman, he says, thinks she is somebody else in the hands of a stronger power.

"She thinks she is under superhuman control. She is compelled to do things by spirits. She hears a command, partly in her dream, that she must carry out. Sometimes it takes the form of voices in which she is commanded to steal, to murder, or to confess things she never did, and she has no peace of mind until she makes a confession of something she has never done. The torture is something violent until she confesses that which she has not done.

"Imagines she is pursued. Imagines that she has stolen something, or that somebody thinks she has stolen something, and fears the law. She hears voices and warnings, and in the night she dreams about it. The state of torture is something dreadful, and it then goes into a delirium with muttering. The delirium is carried on like one muttering when drunk. This state increases until unconsciousness comes on and the patient enters into a coma from which he cannot be aroused. The patient also goes through periods of violence and violent delirium."

Besides hay fever and a number of other ailments, lachesis is extremely useful in the diseases of alcoholics, everything from red noses to liver problems. If the doctor had prescribed lachesis rather than pulsatilla for my own complaints and I had read the above account, my reaction would not have been a happy one. Perhaps this is why homoeopaths are so reluctant to disclose their medicines to patients.

2,000 Remedies

There are about 2,000 homoeopathic remedies, and their ingredients are made from plants, metals, and animal substances. Alcohol, which is sometimes advocated by allopathic doctors as being therapeutic in small doses, is never used in homoeopathic medicines (except as a solvent). Marijuana, however, is, especially for the disease of gonorrhoea. The description of the drug, technically known as *cannabis indica*, in the *Materia Medica*, is: "A strange ecstatic sensation pervades the body and senses. The limbs and parts seem enlarged. A thrill of beatitude passes over the limbs. The limbs tremble. Great weakness spreads over the body. The symptoms resemble catalepsy. Anaesthesia and loss of muscular sense. Complaints ameliorated by rest. Exaltation of spirits with mirthfulness.

"Wonderful imaginations and hallucinations. Wonderful exaggerations of time and space. He seems to be transported through space. He seems to have two existences, or to be conscious of two states, or to exist in two spheres. Delusions. Incoherent speech. Laughs at serious remarks. Laughs and weeps. Spasmodic laughter. Jesting. Moaning and weeping. Fear of death; of insanity; of the dark. Anguish and sadness.

"Mental symptoms ameliorated by walking in the open air. An opposite phase prevails with his weakness. He loses his senses and falls. Passes from the rational to the irrational in rapid succession, back and forth. Forgets words and ideas. Unable to finish his sentences. Thoughts crowding upon each other in such confusion prevent rational speech.

"His mind is full of unfinished ideas, and phantoms. Wonderful theories constantly form in the mind. Loquacity. He cannot control the mind to reason rationally upon any subject. Any effort to reason is interrupted by flights of wild imagination and theory. Vision upon vision passes before the perception. Hears voices, bells, music, in ecstatic confusion."

The drug is used for gonorrhoea because it produces symptoms of increased sexual desire as well as frequent urination. The homoeopathic dosage is, of course, infinitesimal, and does not produce the state described above.

Taking the Case
In prescribing homoeopathic remedies, says Dr Close, to quote again from his *Genius of Homoeopathy,* the doctor must study his patient as an individual. And this principle of individualization must apply equally in three departments:

"1. The examination of the patient. This must be conducted in such a manner as to bring out all the facts of the case. Each symptom, as far as possible, must be rendered complete in the three elements of locality, sensation, and modality, or conditions of existence.

"2. The examination of the symptom-record of the patient or the 'study of the case.' This must be made in such a manner as to determine what symptoms represent that which is curable by medication under the law of similars; in other words, to determine, in each particular case, what symptoms have a counterpart in the materia medica.

"3. The examination of the materia medica by means of indexes, repertories, etc., for the purpose of discovering that remedy which, in its symptomatology, is most similar to the symptoms of the individual patient at a particular time."

Hahnemann's greatness is unquestioned, even by those who most resent his theories. First, he was the earliest physician to join biology and psychology with physics in a practical system of healing.

Second, he formulated the concepts of dynamis and the life force with their relation to health.

Third, he experimented with the action of drugs upon healthy human subjects, observing the subjective as well as objective phenomena. In so doing, he was the pioneer of a whole new field of research and a new art of medicine and psychology.

According to Dr Close: "The philosophy of Hahnemann is based upon and includes not only the physiological and pathological actions and reactions of man as a physical organism, but of man as spiritual and psychical being; for it includes and utilizes the mental, the subjective and the functional phenomena as they are developed under the influence of hygeopoietic and pathogenetic agencies.

"In this respect homoeopathy differs radically from and is infinitely superior to all other systems of therapeutics; and this is solely because it recognizes Life or Mind as an entity; as the primary, spiritual power or principle which creates and sustains the physical organism and is the primary cause of all its actions and reactions. Its working principle is the universal Law of Reciprocal Action, otherwise known as the law of balance, compensation, rhythm, polarity, vibration, or action and reaction, all of which signify a principle operative alike in the physical, mental and spiritual realms. In its out-working it is essentially the *Law of Love*, for it is always beneficent, always creative, always harmonizing.

"Hence, the consistent practitioner of homoeopathy never uses, and has no need to use, any irritating, weakening, depressing, infecting, intoxicating or injurious agent of any kind in the treatment of the sick, nor to violate the integrity of the body by forcibly introducing medicinal agents by other than the natural orifices and channels.

"Homoeopathy achieves its ends and accomplishes its purposes by the use of single, simple, pure drugs; refined and deprived of their injurious properties and enhanced in curative power by the pharmacodynamical processes of mechanical comminution, trituration, solution and dilution according to scale; in minimum or infinitesimal doses, administered by the mouth; the remedy having been selected by comparison of the symptoms of the sick with the symptoms of drugs produced by tests in healthy human subjects; under the principle of symptom – similarity, as enunciated in the maxims, '*Similia, Similibus Curantur – Simplex, Simile, Minimum.*' (Like will be cured by the like – a like remedy in minimum dose.)"

Spiritual Nature of Healing

Hahnemann, known to admirers as the Old Master, recognized that health and disease involve more than germs and germicides; more than serums and vaccines. He seemed to believe that the true nature of all healing was spiritual. Implicit in this idea was his concept of the vital force.

In his *Organon* he writes: "The material organism, without the vital force, is capable of no sensation, no function, no self-preservation; it derives all sensation and performs all the functions of life solely by means of the immaterial being (the vital principle) which animates the material organism in health and in disease.

"When a person falls ill, it is only this spiritual, self-acting (automatic) vital force, everywhere present in his organism, that is primarily deranged by the dynamic influence upon it of a morbific agent inimical to life; it is only the vital principle, deranged to such an abnormal state, that can furnish the organism with its disagreeable sensations, and incline it to the irregular processes which we call disease; for, as a power invisible in itself, and only cognizable by its effects on the organism, its morbid derangement only makes itself known by the manifestation of disease in the sensations and functions of those parts of the organism exposed to the senses of the observer and physician, that is, by *morbid symptoms*, and in no other way can it make itself known.

"It is the morbidly affected vital energy alone that produces diseases, so that the morbid phenomena perceptible to our senses express at the same time all the internal change, that is to say, the whole morbid derangement of the internal dynamis; in a word, they reveal the whole disease; also, the disappearance under treatment of all the morbid phenomena and of all the morbid alterations that differ from the healthy vital operations, certainly affects and necessarily implies the restoration of the integrity of the vital force and, therefore, the recovered health of the whole organism."

Hahnemann was also a great defender of Mesmer's animal magnetism. "This curative force," he wrote in the *Organon*, "often so stupidly denied ... acts in different ways. It is a marvellous, priceless gift of God to mankind by means of which the strong will of a well-intentioned person upon a sick one by contact and even without ... and even at some distance, can bring the vital energy of the healthy mesmerizer endowed with this power into another person dynamically (just as one of the poles of a powerful magnetic rod upon a bar of steel)."

Animal magnetism, he said, strengthens a patient's vital force when it is weak; it also redistributes such force in cases where it has become too concentrated.

Homoeopathy is, it seems, far more than a system of medicine. It is philosophy, science, and art all rolled into one. Perhaps this is why homoeopathic doctors, who are all fully trained as allopaths, all M.D.s, consider it the most extensive as well as the most difficult type of healing. At present, homoeopathy is most often used by patients as a last resort, allopathy being the first. Many feel this practice will one day be reversed. Of one thing we can be sure. Homoeopathy, in some mysterious way, treats the body as energy rather than mass.

7

D.D. PALMER AND CHIROPRACTIC

Chiropractic is usually defined as a therapeutic system based on the premise that disease is caused by abnormal functioning of the nervous system. The chiropractor attempts to restore normal functioning by manipulation of the spine.

The nervous system, which consists of brain, spinal cord, and nerve branches, controls the interaction and operation of all the body's systems. The health of one's nerves, therefore, has far-reaching effects.

The nervous system may go awry when vertebrae go out of alignment, a situation known as subluxations, which can result from accidents, bad posture, stress, congenital structure, and even improper diet. When the chiropractor adjusts the vertebrae, interference is removed from the nerves. And the body's own healing energy, now unblocked, is allowed to flow.

In spite of what many doctors still say to the contrary, the practice works. I know, because I've been seeing chiropractors off and on for the past ten years, and have found that a skilful adjustment not only relieves back pain but seems to revitalize the entire system. The response from the uninitiated to this statement is usually, "Well, if you have to keep on seeing them, they can't be very effective. Obviously, they haven't been able to solve your problem."

The answer to this is that for me, at least, chiropractic care is a matter of maintenance and preventive medicine. It is my belief that subluxations interfere with health directly and in ways that are still unknown.

Usually, after having a competent adjustment, I feel a rush of energy surging up and down my back; it is rather like being recharged, and it seems to affect my mental as well as my physical health. For this reason, I have long been convinced that chiropractic must be closely associated with the healing energy. Many of the chiropractors I spoke to about this, however, are very pragmatic about their work; and they attribute the feeling of energy to mere relief from nerve pressure.

Nonetheless, I have always believed that there must be something more complex at work, and I finally found that something beautifully explained in a book called *The Chiropractic Story* by Marcus Bach.

Vital Force Called 'Innate'

Here, I discovered that D.D. Palmer, generally credited with the founding of chiropractic in 1895, believed in a vital force or energy, which he called Innate. This Innate was the power that kept the automatic system functioning, and it expressed itself through the nervous system. He also described it as "a segment of that Intelligence which fills the universe." Vertebral adjustments release Innate and work in co-operation with it to effect the cure.

Interested in magnetic healing as well, Palmer wrote, as quoted by Bach, "All observers realize that we are surrounded with an aura; that we pass from our bodies a subtle, invisible substance known as magnetism; that this emanation may be either repellent or attractive. Heat, magnetism, odour, and, no doubt, other unseen forces emanate from our bodies in all directions. It is said that each nationality has its peculiar odour, which, although not recognized by themselves, is readily detected by others. Some persons give off an effluvium that is nauseating, sickening to those who inhale it. Effluvia may be pathologic or physiologic. By this odour, aroma, essence, or scent which emanates or exhales from persons, dogs know their masters, hounds distinguish one person from another or trail their prey for miles.

"There is an emanation from us, not magical or miraculous, but a subtle, invisible substance, capable of perception, which consciously or unconsciously magnetizes, influences, more or less, every person and object with which we come in contact. The rooms we occupy, the furniture used, the food and water handled are more or less permeated with, and become a part of it."

Palmer apparently believed that this energy-giving life to the body was actually nerve force; that it was generated in the cells of the brain and the spinal cord and then sent out through the system of nerves to give power to the organs, as electricity is sent out through wires to furnish light, power, and heat. His goal was to prove that disease of any organ may arise from defects of the nerve centres, rather than from the organ itself.

"Life," he said, "is that vital force which some regard as physical and others as spiritual. It is manifested by the employment of the senses and voluntary movement. Molecular alterations, tissue change, accomplished by an intelligent vital force, constitute a living being. To live, necessitates the possession of life. Life possesses an integence which pervades the universe and is expressed in accordance with the environment and the quality of the material in which it manifests itself.

"What is that which is present in the living body and absent in the dead? It is not inherent. It is not in any of the organs which are essential to life. An intelligent force which I saw fit to name Innate, usually known as Spirit, creates and continues life when vital organs are in a condition to be acted upon by it. This intelligent life-force uses the material of the universe in proportion as it is in a condition to be utilized."*

Chiropractic Does Not Cure

Palmer emphasized that chiropractic does not cure; the adjustment relieves, removes the cause; then the life force (Innate) transmits the impulses without hindrance and effects the cure.

According to author Bach, medicine should catch up with chiropractic in its knowledge of the mechanics of the spine and its premise that the body, including the blood circulation, is controlled through the nervous system. But in order to fully understand chiropractic, traditional medicine must also educate itself in the science of spinal adjustment and in the philosophy of a vital force (or healing energy or Innate).

These two concepts continue to be steeped in riducule born largely out of ignorance. There is much controversy even among chiropractors over the principle of Innate. To some, this life force is nerve energy; to others, consciousness; to some, electrical impulse; to others, nature; to some, God in man.

Most people believe that chiropractic was born on September 18, 1895, in Davenport, Iowa, when D.D. Palmer adjusted the vertebra of

* From *The Chiropractic Story* by Marcus Bach.

a deaf janitor named Harvey Lillard, whose hearing was restored as a result. Others say chiropractics is simply the rebirth of Hippocrates's rachiotherapy.

D.D. Palmer wrote in his book, *The Chiropractor's Adjuster*, "The basic principles of chiropractic are not new. They are as old as the vertebrata. ... I do claim, however, to be the first to replace displaced vertebrae by using the spinous and transverse processes as levers ... and from this basic fact to create a science which is destined to revolutionize the theory and practice of the healing art."

Kleanthes A. Ligeros, M.D., Ph.D., of Athens, claims that all of mankind has in some way since the Stone Age practised some form of spinal manipulation. Massage and the laying on of hands, he writes in his book, *How Ancient Healing Governs Modern Therapeutics*, are universal, instinctive types of therapy.

According to Ligeros, "chiropraxy" was known to the Greeks more than 32 centuries ago; and the ancient Egyptians, Chinese, and Hindus left concise but clear descriptions of this art.

Paralyzed Fingers

Galen, too, in the second century A.D., reportedly revived the paralyzed fingers of the scholar, Eudemus, by treating the nerves in his neck. When dissecting an ape in the school at Alexandria, he had investigated the connection between the nerves of the neck and the spinal column. After learning that Eudemus had once been thrown from a chariot and suffered a blow to his neck, Galen applied his knowledge.

The ancient *kahunas* also used chiropractic techniques in order to stimulate the healing energy known as *mana*.

Ligeros continues: " ... the principles embodied in modern chiropractic, orthopaedic surgery, osteopathy, and podiatry long have been known to man, and particularly to the Hellenes.

"Much authentic information indicative of the existence of applied spinal and body mechanics in ancient Hellas has reached us today. Such knowledge, coming from indisputable masters, teaches us that in the classical times of Greece, body mechanics, spinal balancing, and vertebral adjusting were thoroughly investigated, understood and applied long before the Hippocratean epoch.

The relationship of the vertebral column to the nervous system and to the human frame, as well as to the different diseases of the living organism, were adequately recognized and sufficiently investigated, and also demonstrated by them. Furthermore, they have, so to say, providentially included most of such valuable observations and conclusions in their many notable writings.

"From these works it becomes evident that every possible angle in regard to spinal function and derangement has been well investigated, exploited and treated at great length by them. Deliberately or otherwise, the Hellenes efficiently detected not only the various malformations and displacements, curvatures and other distortions of the human frame, particularly the spinal column, but much to our amazement they even discovered the slightest misalignments of the different vertebrae which are often displaced or slightly luxated, or rather subluxated.

"Only to think that modern medicine with all its remarkable advancement has failed thus far to appreciate fully the ancient scientific facts about partial luxations of the vertebral segments and the various other spinal conditions and factors which seriously affect the organism, is to wonder how Hippocrates was able to detect, without the aid of precision instruments, X-rays, etc., even the slightest vertebral displacements and to note their ill effects upon the whole organism.

"Hippocrates more than once called the attention of the practitioner to these truths, admonishing him, as well as the prospective student, to endeavour to learn to comprehend well the nature of the spinal column, to study closely its structure and, so to say, functions. Such study, he advised, is necessary in many diseases."

Mechanism of Spinal Column
Ligeros believes that Hippocrates studied the mechanism of the spinal column and thoroughly understood its importance.

"He appears to have known well its relation and application to and effects upon the nervous system, and also its influence upon the whole organism. He described its mechanical maleffects upon the soft tissues adjacent to the spine, as make them tense and taut and somewhat elevated to the touch.

He insisted that the practitioner should become well acquainted with all these facts, and learn the mechanical relation of the spinal column to the nervous system and of the latter to the organism, so as to be ever ready to make proper correction in case of such skeletal and spinal displacements and malformations or similar derangements, by means of reduction, extension, counter-extension, succession, etc. He described various methods and mechanical appliances as well as the vathron, which is the modern surgeon's orthopaedic chair or chiropractic table or bench."

It was mentioned in the third chapter that Hippocrates felt the role of the physician was to remove the causes of illness – so that the healing power of nature, the *vis medicatrix naturae*, could cure the patient. It should be emphasized that Palmer said the same thing, only his name for the curative force was Innate.

Chiropractic Theory

John F. Thie, D.C., in his book, *Touch for Health*, written with Mary Marks, describes chiropractic theory as the belief that the innate intelligence that runs the body is connected to a universal intelligence that runs the world; and each person is plugged into the universal intelligence through the nervous system.

"It is the job of the chiropractor," he writes, "to help this communication system, to insure that the body will function. He does this by working with the spine, the central core of the nervous system, the master system of the body. Then the body can take care of itself because there is no interference between the intelligences and the body."

Dr Thie, like many chiropractors, is also interested in a new system called applied kinesiology, developed during the 1960s by Dr George Goodheart of Detroit, Michigan. Applied kinesiology involves muscle tests that are able to evaluate the normal and abnormal function of the body. A weak muscle indicates not only poor function of that muscle, but also possible trouble with the organ and other tissue in the same nerve, vascular, or nutrition grouping. This premise, combined with conventional chiropractic and acupuncture techniques, has caused a new kind of therapy to evolve.

Applied Kinesiology Investigated

In order to investigate the theory, I made appointments with two different chiropractors, one in Connecticut and one in New York. They both used applied kinesiology techniques in evaluating my muscle strengths. Both told me that there was a weakness in my gall bladder meridian, which might or might not mean a gall bladder problem. The first chiropractor gave me a raw liver concentrate, which he said would strengthen the weakness, and he then attempted to adjust my spine. His adjustments were unsatisfactory, and I left his office wishing that he'd concentrate on developing more skilful chiropractic techniques and forget about the kinesiology.

Chiropractor Number Two, however, restored my faith. He was able to use the new system *and* give successful adjustments. Since I've had a neck problem for years, I know that a good chiropractor can give me an adjustment that will usually last for at least a month, and I tend to be wary of those who expect weekly visits. There is a great range of skill and individual excellence among these practitioners, as there is among all groups, and anyone seeking chiropractic help should shop around before settling on the person of his choice.

I have seen about ten chiropractors in the same number of years. Three have been excellent, five fair, and two ineffectual. This is, of course, my own opinion; others might have rated them differently.

Chiropractic history has been stormy. Fighting accusations of quackery and the American Medical Association's unsuccessful attempts to put them out of business, chiropractors have persevered, and their list of grateful patients is overwhelming. In spite of the philosophical infighting that exists within the profession itself − sometimes called a fight between the 'straights' and the 'mixers' − there can be little doubt that chiropractic is growing.

Even experienced yogis, who recognize the importance of the spine and nervous system, acknowledge the need for chiropractors. Mahatma Gandhi used one; and medicine of the future (to be discussed in Chapter 12) will frequently combine the use of yoga and chiropractic.

Chiropractors, especially the younger ones, are holistic in their approach to healing. Dr Thie, for example, who trains people in the use of muscle balancing techniques and the health of the whole person, describes man as a structural, chemical, and psychological or spiritual being.

Dr Thie says: "The primary structure and the natural chemistry operate together to dictate the psychology and vice-versa. Man's problems can be segmented into different systems − structural and neurological, lymphatic, vascular, cerebro-spinal, nutritional and chemical, and meridian systems. A problem may exist in any part of some area, and disturbances in the other systems may represent the body's efforts to compensate for the troubled system."

Vitamin Deficiencies

The nutritional and metabolic state of the body has the utmost effect upon the nervous system, which is why chiropractors display such interest in their patients' diets. Vitamin deficiencies, especially the Bs, may cause widespread degeneration of peripheral nerves, damage to neurons in the brain, and degeneration of spinal cord tracts.

Dr Linus Pauling of Stanford University; twice winner of the Nobel Prize, has written that "the functioning of the brain and nervous tissue is more sensitively dependent on the rate of chemical reactions than the functioning of other organs and tissues. I believe that mental disease is for the most part caused by abnormal reaction rates, as determined by genetic constitution and diet, and by abnormal molecular concentrations of essential substances."

And as long ago as 1952, Aldous Huxley wrote: "The nervous system is more vulnerable than any other tissues of the body; consequently, vitamin deficiencies tend to affect the state of mind before they affect, at least in any very obvious way, the skin, bones, mucous membranes, muscles and viscera. The first result of an inadequate diet is a lowering of the efficiency of the brain as an instrument for biological survival."

It is not surprising that so many chiropractors show such interest in megavitamin therapy. Also, there are a growing number of MDs – about 200 in the United States – who advocate orthomolecular medicine, which combines biochemical and nutritional techniques aimed at providing the optimum molecular environment for the functioning of the mind.

According to the Huxley Institute for Biosocial Research, orthomolecular psychiatry reduces abnormally high levels of toxic substances present in the bodies of mentally disturbed persons and maintains them on nutritional programmes that compensate for inherited biochemical imbalances unique to them.

No one fully understands the human nervous system. It is generally acknowledged as the seat of consciousness and is often compared to a computer complex. Palmer believed the life force, or Innate, was generated in the brain and spinal cord, then sent out, like electricity, through a network of nerves.

The nervous system itself is so extensive and complex that it constitutes on its own, without any other tissues, bones, or organs, a complete three-dimensional human shape. It weighs 1.5 kilograms.

The Mysterious Brain

The brain is the most mystifying of all organs, and no satisfactory model of it exists. A shell or cortex, which is grey, covers a mass of white matter; within this are the basal ganglia and the thalamus, commonly referred to as grey matter; these are cell relay stations that interconnect with one another and the cortex.

The greater part of the brain is made up of the right and left cerebral hemispheres, below which is the brain stem. And behind the stem is the cerebellum. From the brain stem there originate 12 cranial nerves, and from the spinal cord, which is continuous with the stem, there are 31 pairs of mixed nerves that run to all parts of the body. These nerves supply all the muscles of the body except those of the head and some of the neck. They also return sensory impulses to the brain.

The nerves pass from the spinal cord to the body through holes called intervertebral foramina. According to Kelly Snodgrass in her article, 'Chiropractic,' which appeared in the August 1976 issue of *East West Journal*, the foramina are crucial, affecting the physical integrity and spiritual potential of a human being in a multitude of ways, some of which have not been imagined.

"Because they are the result of the relationship between two separate bones, one above the other, the foramina are not rigid. The spine is constructed to be both strong and flexible. During the course of a day there is a continual alteration of the size and shape of the invertebral foramina as the body moves and twists, and even in the stillness of rest the breath expands and contracts in a gentler flow. Body movement produces a gentle pulsing around the nerves as they pass through the foramina to form the intricate network of the nervous system."

The foraminal environment, the article continues, can be thrown off by poor diet, since faulty nutrition probably produces body imbalance. "The unbalanced expansion or contraction of body tissues might express itself as nerve interference by affecting muscles or changing the nature of the foraminal environment. A body built on the typical American diet will require years of natural eating to counteract years of improper eating, and in the meantime chiropractic can help free the body to deal with the effects of a previously poor diet while using the elements of the improved diet for maximum benefit."

The foramina are buried beneath layers of skin, muscle, and bone, and are, therefore inaccessible. The chiropractor cannot examine them, so he examines the vertebrae instead. If the bones are properly related, he assumes that the foramina are not interfering with the normal nerve function. If, however, the vertebrae are out of alignment and a subluxation exists, he assumes that the foramina are also 'fixed,' thus causing problems for the nerves passing through them.

Nerve Circuits

The nerve circuits of the body fall into two groups. Those whose centres lie in the brain or spinal cord form the cerebrospinal or central nervous system. Those whose centres lie on each side of the backbone and among the chief organs form the autonomic or sympathetic nervous system.

In general it may be said that the central system controls relations of the body with the outside world; it is responsible for touch, sight, taste, hearing, smell, and feelings of heat and cold. The autonomic system is responsible for our internal processes: the beating of the heart, the circulation of the blood, the movements of the stomach and intestines, the work of the glands, and other functions that perform without any conscious effort on our part.

The two systems are connected by nerve fibres in the spinal cord. These connections produce the close interaction between the two systems – as exemplified by the blush upon embarrassment, the tears of sadness, or the rapid heartbeat of excitement.

The hypothalamus, the part of the brain that lies below the thalamus, controls the autonomic system and is often referred to as the 'old brain' that we share with the lower forms of life. According to Dr Irving Oyle in *The Healing Mind*, it is a biocomputer that monitors and regulates heart rate, blood-pressure, chemical balance, and every vital function beyond the will.

"It is also," he writes, "the seat of the emotions which it creates and regulates through a complex network of nerves and hormones. Receiving impulses from both cerebral hemispheres, it converts information into bodily states (as in the fight-or-flight reaction, or sexual arousal). It also controls the body's system of defence. This magnificent computer is controlled and programmed by the cerebral cortical brain, consciously or unconsciously.

"*Cancer, arthritis, heart disease, and stroke are likely to be bodily states induced by an unconscious command or picture of self-destruction.* The female, form-creating hemisphere contains the body image. It communicates by means of unconscious gestures, smiles, frowns, raised eyebrows, and the like. Since it shares control over the body through the hypothalamic computer, perhaps it can induce healing in case of faulty programming or disease."

The female, form-creating hemisphere referred to by Dr Oyle is, of course, the right, subconscious one referred to in Chapter 2. The left hemisphere, the reasoner, is considered male. And ease, as opposed to disease, occurs when the two are in harmony — a kind of mystical, hermaphroditic marriage, during which the healing energy is released.

The two hemispheres of the brain are an integral part of the nervous system — and chiropractic treats the nervous system. One day science may discover that subluxations have been the cause of many mental as well as physical disturbances. And when that time comes, healers will undoubtedly repeat Hippocrates's famous dictum: "In the case of disease, look to the spine."

8

WAS REICH RIGHT?

Wilhelm Reich, a psychiatrist and natural scientist, was convinced that he had found the secret of all creation in what he called orgone energy, a mass-free primordial power that operates throughout the universe as the basic life force.

Reich described this energy as being present in all living things, as well as in the atmosphere and soil. He said that the proper flow of this force throughout the body was essential to health. He believed that the sun produced this energy and that it was related to variations in the earth's magnetism. It could also, he said, be measured electrically or by thermometer and was visible as a blue-gray radiation on colour film.

He believed the energy to be intelligent. It was also, he conjectured, the scientific reality of what most people call God.

Although Wilhelm Reich is considered by many to have been one of the world's great innovative thinkers, history has yet to pay him homage. For in spite of his distinguished contributions to science, many of his ideas were regarded as outrageous and even dangerous nonsense. Discredited by the U.S. government in 1956, his discoveries were dismissed as quackery; his books were burned; and Reich himself was sent to prison. He died on November 3, 1957, in the federal penitentiary at Lewisburg, Pa.

In many respects, this extraordinary man's career resembles a larger-than-life mystery drama with most of the questions still unsolved: did he really learn to harness the all-encompassing life force, which he named orgone energy? Was he a madman as well as a genius? Was his final disgrace arranged by an outside conspiracy, as he claimed, or was he paranoid, as others claimed? The riddle of Reich persists as one of the most fascinating dilemmas of the century, for it involves, also, the riddle of the universe.

Born in Austria on March 24, 1897, Reich was the son of a wealthy farmer, and his boyhood surroundings were conducive to an early study of agriculture and animal behaviour.

Brilliant Disciple of Freud

After earning his M.D. from the University of Vienna in 1922, he soon became known as one of Freud's most brilliant disciples. Although he was a highly respected psychoanalyst in Vienna throughout the 1920s, his extreme views gradually began to alienate his colleagues.

Enlarging upon Freud's libido theory, which had finally achieved a dubious respectability, Reich decided that all neuroses were caused by sexual blockages; he said that a fully successful orgasm – one, he seemed to imply, that involved the mind-body-spirit – would release the sexual energy and eliminate the neurosis. He also claimed that the muscular rigidity, or 'armouring,' which he had observed consistently in the mentally ill, was caused by sexual stasis and inhibited the body's natural flow of energy.

His technique for loosening this armour in order to release the blocked emotions involved certain exercises and breathing therapies from which today's bioenergetics, Rolfing and Gestalt therapies are derived. In the Twenties, a physical rather than psychical approach to neurosis was revolutionary.

Reich regarded the armour (or character armour) as a defence erected by the patient against revealing his unconscious sexual tendencies; the objective of his therapy was to destroy the character armour, thus returning the patient to his proper biological functioning, which involved full 'potency.' The credibility of his theory has consistently suffered from the fact that many highly disturbed and even psychotic individuals are capable of full orgastic potency.

Orson Bean, however, in his book, *Me and the Orgone*, both clarifies and defends Reich's point of view:

Healthy Sex Drive

"In the healthy, unarmoured, self-regulated person, the whole process of sex is quite different from the way it is with an armoured person. In the healthy person, the sex drive is not separated from love but is, rather, the physical counterpart of it. The truly self-regulated person never uses sex for self-aggrandizement or power or control or subjugation. Rather, he feels it as an overpowering need to melt into another, to become physically one with his love object.

He is filled with tenderness and caring and concern for his partner at the height of the sex act. The world falls away and indeed they do become one for the moment, for at orgasm, true orgasm, the energy fields of the partners fuse and merge as the excess energy is released through the genitals.

Any idea of using, or humiliating, or degrading ... the partner is alien and unthinkable, and afterwards the feeling is one of love and tenderness and deep gratitude.

"In neurotic, armoured people, sexual strivings are felt through deadened and hardened muscles. The soft, warm, tender glow felt by the self-regulated person is absent and in its place is a desperate feeling of wanting to 'break out' of one's own body. For the armoured person, the sex act seems to be filled with danger. All the old childish anxieties come up with the sexual excitation: the mixed feelings, the guilt, the castration fears. To 'succeed' becomes the end-all of the act ...

Fantasies are employed to overcome the anxieties that make completion of the act impossible. But the fantasies make the act unreal and destroy any feeling of tenderness and finally when the desperate grinding is over there is the inevitable letdown, the feeling of self-loathing and disgust and 'what's the meaning of it all?' "

Aside from what his colleagues considered to be an obsession with the role of sex in neurosis, Reich also became involved with radical politics and in his writings tried to bridge the gap between Freud and Marx. He horrified his peers by stating that the antisexual, puritanical mores of Western society have so restricted people's orgastic ability that only the rare individual is capable of full potency. It was therefore, he said, the task of psychoanalysis to revive the orgastic ability of humankind. His outspokenness alienated him, naturally, from both his professional and political colleagues. Forced to leave Vienna, he then shocked the populaces of Berlin, Copenhagen, and Oslo.

In 1939, while still in Norway, he enraged almost everyone by announcing his discovery of orgone energy, a vital energy, which, he said, regulated the health of living creatures and permeated the entire universe.

The press attacked him mercilessly. He was labelled a sex pervert, a 'creator of life,' and was expelled from the International Psychoanalytic Association.

Seeking a more open environment, he came to the U.S., where he took a teaching and lecturing position at the New School for Social Research.

Never content to be one more rich, successful psychoanalyst, Reich's heart was always in scientific research and discovery.

He often spoke of a 'red thread' of logic that led him from one step to the next. His biologic basis for Freud's libido theory stimulated his discovery of bioenergetic functions; this triggered the development of the orgasm theory, which in turn led to the discovery of the life-energy or orgone energy.

Reich believed that the tingling feeling experienced during sexual excitement was a manifestation of orgone energy in the body. After finding this force in human beings, he sought it in nature, in the atmosphere, and eventually in outer space. He came to believe that unidentified flying objects (UFOs) were space ships fuelled by orgone energy.

Bions

Reich, from all reports, was tireless and meticulous in his laboratory work. Six years before he announced the discovery of orgone energy, he had detected basic units of living matter, which he called bions, under the microscope.

By dropping particles of carbon into a filtered solution of bouillon and potassium chloride, he said the bions, which were blue, would appear and cause the heavy carbon particles to change their nature and become living matter.

He first confronted orgone energy after examining seasand cultures regularly under the microscope. Finding that they hurt his eyes and skin, he concluded that the cultures were giving off some form of radiation. Tests for radioactivity, however, proved negative. He also noted that, in the dark, the cultures gave off a bluish light, and objects charged with this blue energy could influence an electroscope.

Reich constructed a box to contain the energy. It had metal walls and layers of organic matter outside, which would absorb any energy that managed to penetrate the metal. He observed a bluish light around the cultures in this box. And this light, he noted, remained even after the cultures had been removed.

The 'box,' Reich decided, had been picking up orgone energy in its outer layer and transmitting it through the metal walls, where it was contained like heat in a greenhouse. This was the origin of Reich's orgone box, which one of his disciples has described as the greatest discovery ever made by medical science.

The orgone box is an energy accumulator, said Reich, and if sick people sit beside one, they can quickly be 'recharged.' If they sit too long, they will develop symptoms similar to sunstroke.

More than anything else, he hoped for an endorsement of his discoveries by Einstein. Experimenting with cancerous mice, he found that those spending half an hour per day in the accumulator lived much longer than the others. Although he claimed no cure for cancer, Reich believed these observations might parallel Einstein's theories on the relationship between matter and energy.

Meeting with Einstein

He wrote to Einstein, and a meeting was arranged in January 1941. In a letter to his friend, A.S. Neill, founder of the well-known Summerhill School, Reich said that Einstein admitted to seeing the orgone energy with the use of the orgonoscope – an instrument Reich devised to see the flickering of the orgone – but then wondered if his eyes were playing tricks on him.

Reich also said that Einstein kept the accumulator for several days in order to test certain observations of temperature change. And although he noted the same things that Reich had, Einstein attributed them to different causes. When Reich sent further proof of his discoveries, Einstein ignored it.

Since the above is based almost entirely on one letter, there is no way of knowing, unfortunately, the full story of the Reich-Einstein exchange.

Feeling rebuffed by orthodox science, Reich nevertheless continued his research, moving his laboratory from New York to Rangeley, Me. Opposed to the mechanistic specialization in the various fields of science, he was convinced that his energy concept unified the various disciplines into one functional body.

Reich believed that the confusion existing in the realm of nuclear physics was due to the mechanistic thinking of its investigators. Problems at the subatomic* level, he said, would only make sense when approached 'orgonomically,' that is, with an understanding of orgone energy. His approach, then, to understanding the secrets of the universe was through a process of orgonomic** rather than

---

* Relating to the phenomena occurring inside atoms or particles smaller than atoms.

** In describing this process, Reich usually substituted the word functional for orgonomic. The latter is used here for clarity.

mechanical reasoning. The difference between these is described in his book, *Ether, God and Devil*. The subject is certainly worth probing, since Reich emphasized repeatedly that this was the key that would open the door to an understanding of modern physics.

Since Reich's death, physics, as a science, has become increasingly enigmatic. In *The Tao of Physics*, Fritjof Capra explores the parallels between modern physics and Eastern mysticism. The link between this science and para-psychology is, in fact, articulated repeatedly and persuasively.

The Quantum Theory

Certainly there can be little doubt that the quantum theory has annihilated conventional concepts of solid objects and, even certain long-accepted laws of nature. For at the subatomic level, the solid material objects of classical physics dissolve into wave-like patterns that are both unpredictable and indeterminate.

In April 1976, John Wheeler of Princeton, one of the architects of modern physics, cited what he considers to be one of the greatest challenges to science: why quantum behaviour pervades natural phenomena; why such phenomena on the level of atoms, molecules, and radiation occur in discrete bursts and sudden changes of state rather than in a continuous manner. Wheeler postulated that the ultimate reality may be as chaotic as Jackson Pollock's unstructured paintings.

Reich, had he lived, would undoubtedly have repeated his premise that the ultimate reality would never appear to be logical or intelligible without an understanding of orgone energy.

Reich believed in an orgonic view of life that was opposed to an atomic one. The atomic view, which was also the chemical view, he said, was the rule of chemistry monopolies, artificial drugs, unnatural adulterated foods, and noisy, smoky motors.

The OR-Motor (one fuelled by orgone energy) was, Reich said, the first step in the technological development toward "noiseless, smokeless, smooth-functioning locomotor machines of the future. Inevitably, the Cosmic Energy Motor will replace the steam engine and the electrical motor. It will be fed by the practically limitless power resources contained in the Cosmic Orgone Energy Ocean. It will be the motor that will carry our spaceships into vastnesses as yet unimaginable.

"This motor will finally and irretrievably free man from the so very futile effort of overcoming gravity by way of mechanical thrust, the jet-engine type of motor function. Both mechanical gravity, theoretical gravity and the machine to carry its own gravity field with itself, the Cosmic Energy Field will be ours in a not too far remote future ... The Cosmic Energy Motor will be the lever which will turn our present civilization into that of the coming *Cosmic Age*."*

Some of Reich's assertions, like the above, tend to leave one rather breathless. His language was extravagant, like that of Paracelsus, and it is not difficult to understand why he was so frequently regarded as 'odd.'

Radio-Activity and Orgone

In 1950, while in Rangeley, Me., Reich investigated orgone energy in regard to the control of nuclear radiation. He had observed an antagonism between radio-activity and the orgone, and he hoped that might uncover a defence against harmful radiation. After purchasing some radioactive isotopes from the Atomic Energy Commission, he put them into the large accumulator in his laboratory.

The orgone, however, instead of weakening the radioactivity, did the opposite. The isotopes became excited and spread their radiation far beyond the accumulator. Everyone involved was taken ill, even though they had observed the precautionary measures prescribed by the Atomic Energy Commission.

The experiment, which Reich called the Oranur experiment, was considered a disaster until all those who had become ill not only recovered but, according to Reich, seemed more vigorous than before. He concluded that the orgone energy within living bodies continues to react to nuclear radiation for months and even years.

Reich believed this energy to be more important and more powerful than nuclear energy because it was the force from which atoms were created rather than that caused by thier disintegration. (Atomic energy represents energy freed from matter through splitting the atom, and is a secondary energy *after* matter. Orgone energy is the primordial, mass-free cosmic energy *before* matter.)

The Oranur experiment, said Reich, confirmed the basic antithesis of orgone energy and nuclear energy. This may be illustrated by the following, as listed in Westlake's *Pattern of Health*. (See table overleaf.)

* See *Wilhelm Reich vs. the U.S.A.* by Jerome Greenfield, p. 315.

	Orgone energy	Nuclear energy
In ethics	Good	Evil
In religion	God	Devil
In biology	Life	Death
In bioenergetics	Pa bions	T bions
In physics	Orgone energy	Nuclear energy
In cosmology	Cosmic energy before matter	Cosmic energy after matter

Reich asserted that the Oranur experiment also illuminated those functions that distinguished the orgone from electricity or magnetism. He believed that the energy had behaved 'meaningfully' (in its purposefully negative response to the nuclear radiation) and had indicated the reality of an intelligent universe.

"The sharp boundary lines between physics and what is called metaphysics have broken down," Reich said. "The metaphysical intuition has a physical basis: God and cosmic energy are one. All boundaries between science and religion, science and art, physics and psychology, astronomy and religion, God and ether are of the basic unity, a basic central force which branches out into the various branches of human experience. Cosmic orgone energy is not mystical; it is a basic law of nature."

DOR – Deadly Orgone

After the Oranur experiment, Reich concluded that the orgone energy, when stimulated by nuclear energy, became noxious. He called this form of orgone DOR, deadly orgone. Further investigation led him to believe that DOR was also responsible for air pollution due to nuclear testing, and disease (orgone energy caught in the body, its flow blocked, became DOR and was the primary cause of illness).

Reich, in his desire to counteract DOR, developed an apparatus made of metal pipes that pointed towards the sky. When this was attached to an orgone accumulator grounded in water, he said, it would remove DOR from the atmosphere so that fresh orgone could come in. And a smaller version of this apparatus, he said, would remove DOR from people.

Reich's discovery of DOR and the apparatus for removing it, which he called a cloudbuster, led to his experiments in weather control. More than a decade earlier, Reich had said that cloud formation and thunderstorms were phenomena that had remained unexplained because they were caused by changes in the concentration of atmospheric orgone.

Later, according to Jerome Greenfield in his book, *Wilhelm Reich vs. the U.S.A.*, Reich put forward the idea of an orgone energy envelope surrounding the earth and the possibility that desert formation and droughts were results of stale orgone energy that had turned to DOR within this envelope.

"This and two other formulations constituted the theoretical foundation for extensive work in weather control in which Reich was engaged from the early Fifties until his imprisonment in 1957. One of these principles is that the movement of orgone energy, in defiance of the laws governing other forms of energy, is always from the lower to the higher potential (which is in violation of the second law of thermodynamics and its principle of entropy).* The second is that orgone energy has a strong affinity for water."

Mr Greenfield also quotes several newspapers:

The Rain in Maine

In Maine, the *Bangor Daily News*, July 24, 1953, contained an item called 'Has Maine Scientist Answer to Rainmaking?' It said: "Two men on the verge of losing their crops to the whims of nature took a chance when a scientist told them, 'I think I can give you some rain within 12 to 24 hours.' And the chance paid off ...

"The scientist was Dr Wilhelm Reich, head of the Orgone Institute at Rangeley, Maine, and discoverer of 'orgone energy,' the cosmic life energy of the atmosphere.

"Dr Reich and three assistants set up their 'rainmaking' device off the shore of Grand Lake near Bangor Hydro-Electric dam at 10.30 o'clock, Monday morning, July 6. The device ... conducted a 'drawing' operation for about an hour and 10 minutes ...

"Rain began to fall shortly after 10 o'clock Monday evening, first as a drizzle and then by midnight as a gentle, steady rain. Rain continued throughout the night and a rainfall of 24 inches was recorded in Ellsworth the following morning.

"A puzzled witness ... said, 'The queerest looking clouds you ever saw began to form after they got the thing rolling.'

---

* The second law of thermodynamics concerns the nature of thermal energy (heat) and temperature. It reflects the experience that heat flows from a higher to a lower temperature, but that it does not do the reverse; it is best formulated in terms of entropy (measure of disorder at the molecular and atomic levels).

"Monday, July 13, the drought was broken when heavy rain fell throughout most of the East. A total of 1.74 inches of rainfall was measured in Ellsworth – greater than any other section of the state."

The rainmaking device referred to was, of course, Reich's cloudbuster, which (he said) functioned on the principle of the lightning rod, but controlling orgone energy rather than electrical energy.

In September of 1954, weather experts were convinced that Hurricane Edna would pass over New York and New England. Reich used his apparatus to divert it – and it did change direction. Newscasters attributed the storm's sudden change of course to a miracle.

Cosmic Phenomena

Reich's work, from 1952 on, was referred to as cosmic orgone engineering (CORE). Besides weather control, it involved cosmic phenomena such as outer space and spaceships. His wife, Ilse Ollendorff Reich, in her biography, *Wilhelm Reich*, said that she was not able to understand this new phase of her husband's endeavours. In fact, it was at this point that many of Reich's supporters lost faith in his hold on reality. For Reich believed implicitly in the actuality of extraterrestrials and spaceships.

Earth, he said, was under hostile observation by such craft, and only through the proper use of orgone energy could they be warded off. It was Reich's opinion that the spaceships themselves were propelled by orgone energy, and that the exhaust of their machines produced DOR. He said: "The mechanistic physicists are incapable of coping with the problem. Earth's scientists are not equipped methodically or factually to understand how craft can travel through empty space with such speed and efficiency. Mechanistic, classical physics knows nothing of the Primal Cosmic Energy."

Statements such as these seemed incredible even to his sympathizers, and to his foes he was the mad hatter and mad scientist rolled into one. Yet one year after his death, retired Major Donald Keyhoe said in his book, *Flying Saucers, Top Secret*, that many astronomers had agreed that millions of other worlds must exist, and that some may have civilizations further advanced than our own.

"There is now full proof," he said, "that despite strong efforts to hide the fact, the earth is under close observation by one or more of these advanced worlds. Since the explosion of the first A-bomb, hundreds of officially verified reports, by pilots and other technically trained observers, have proved that intelligently controlled machines, superior to any earthmade craft, are systematically exploring our planet."

Keyhoe added that these "strange machines" had been seen in growing numbers, in direct proportion to our atomic-bomb tests and the launching of artificial satellites and space probes. Keyhoe said that military secrecy dictates the official attitude to be one of debunking "the saucers" and explaining away sightings. But, he states, behind the scenes, a far different attitude exists.

Keyhoe's comments were discredited by most officials, but his view has gained much support in the past decade. It isn't difficult to understand why authorities desired to stifle such information. The panic created years ago by Orson Welles's famous radio play, *The War of the Worlds*, is reason enough. However, it is difficult to understand today why any possible danger from outer space should exceed that which presently exists on earth. When a Princeton student can build a nuclear bomb at small expense, one cannot help but imagine terrorist groups embarking on the same project. And *that* is frightening. If extraterrestrials do indeed exist, they've already had plenty of time to attack us. Perhaps they have transcended the earthling's warlike nature. After all, even on this planet it is only homo sapiens and the ants who engage in organized battle.

Reich's fear of extraterrestrials did little to enhance his reputation for sanity. Nor did his suspicions concerning the Russians.

Soviet Bioplasma

Ever since his youthful romance with Marxism, Reich had become intensely anti-Communist. And he worried that Russia would start using orgone energy before the United States. He knew that the Soviet embassy had ordered a list of all his books in the Forties, and he believed Russian scientists to be more hospitable to new ideas than those in America. His belief that he was being hounded by Communist conspirators has been generally attributed to paranoia. However, the Soviets' recently developed 'bioplasma' bears a striking similarity to Reich's orgone energy.

Ironically enough, the Russians did obtain copies of Reich's books before they were burned, and their psychotronic energy and what they call bioplasma have the same properties as Reich's orgone energy. This is not to say that they could not have come upon their discoveries independently. Reich worried constantly that the Soviet Union would harness this energy before the United States. He seemed especially concerned about its use in the area of weather control.

In a recent issue of the *Saturday Review* (Feb. 5, 1977), an editorial by Norman Cousins discusses the fact that the Central Intelligence Agency (CIA) is presently investigating the weather and its recent trends in regard to cooling, ice cover, floods, and droughts. The CIA report that discusses this subject also points out that national governments are now capable of manipulating weather for military purposes.

"The weather-warfare programmes of the military-scientific establishments of the U.S.A. and the U.S.S.R. are euphemistically known as 'weather modification,'" writes Mr Cousins. "The CIA report does not indicate how far 'W-M' has developed, but the implication is clear that it involves the manufacture of droughts and floods, and is a powerful addition to modern arsenals."

Whether or not these W-M programmes are utilizing the force known as bioplasma or orgone or *ch'i* or others is still an unanswered question, but there can be little doubt that the possibility exists.

"Conspiracy to Kill Orgonomy"

The reality of the orgone energy was severely questioned in relation to Reich's orgone energy accumulators. And in 1947, the U.S. Food and Drug Administration began an investigation into these devices. According to Mr Wyvell, director of publications of the Wilhelm Reich Foundation, the investigation was instigated by "a conspiracy to kill orgonomy and to defame the discoverer of orgone energy ... but the efforts to establish sexual defamation and to claim that the orgone energy accumulator was distributed for profit completely failed, and the conspiracy died out in 1950."

In March of 1954, however, the investigation was revived, and an injunction was served on Reich and his foundation in which "the defendants were enjoined from distribution of orgone energy accumulators ... all accumulators to be disassembled, all printed matter regarding these or orgone energy to be destroyed, on the ground that orgone energy does not exist."

Reich did not answer the complaint because, in his words: "such action would, to my mind, imply the authority of this special branch of government to pass judgment on primordial preatomic energy ... For, if painstaking, elaborated and published scientific findings over a period of 30 years could not convince the administration, or will not be able to convince any other social administration of the true nature of the discovery of the Life Energy, no litigation in any court anywhere will ever hope to do so."

Reich and his co-workers appealed the injunction, but the case was unsuccessful. In May 1956, while pursuing his weather control investigations, Reich was arrested for violation of the injunction. Charged with contempt of court, he received a two-year prison term. In August, all of his scientific books were burned. Fifteen months later, he died in prison of a heart attack.

The true facts concerning Reich's sanity are still unknown, and the validity of orgone energy has yet to be proved. Detractors say his theories were the result of his madness. Yet Reich developed those theories to aid a world that he himself found lunatic. Some say that he was supersane rather than insane. Even friends, however, admit that his behaviour was bizarre towards the end. He was, after all, grappling with laws of the universe as well as those that are man-made – and all against tremendous odds. If orgone energy can ever be authenticated, this strange man's reputation will undoubtedly be resurrected and his position in history turned 'Reich-side-up.'

9

THE HEALING ENERGY OF A MODERN PSYCHIC HEALER

Yolanda B is a psychic and spiritual healer from Rumania, although she is of Hungarian birth. Arriving in the United States in 1969, Mrs B lived first in Florida and now resides in New York. A middle-aged woman who radiates intelligence, strength, and humour, she is one psychic healer whose powers I was able to confront personally.

When interviewing her in the Manhattan apartment where she now lives with her son and daughter-in-law, I had anticipated a conversation, not a first-hand demonstration. Mrs B's power flows through one's feet, which she holds during the healing process, and it was with some trepidation that I removed my boots.

After about ten minutes, Mrs B described my neck problem, personality traits, and even work habits. All of it was true. A few minutes later, I felt a stream of what seemed like cool air flow from her hands. This was, she said, the healing energy for which she was a channel. My reaction to this energy was a sense of well-being that remained with me for some time.

Yolanda B's attitude towards the healing energy is perhaps best described by the following. (Because she has not yet mastered the English language, her statements were partially interpreted by her friend, Joyce Moore, of Pompano Beach, Fla.):

"The most important thing we need to remember in attempting to explain paranormal phenomena is that we cannot separate life from form. Everything that is, is energy – one source ... one source of all life and an infinite variety of expressions of life exist beyond tangibility. We can call this energy life force.

The same energy that flows through rocks, flows through animals, the vegetable kingdom, and flows through each and every one of us. It is that life force that is tapped into, that is harnessed because of the peculiar makeup of a gifted individual, the healer. The healer then acts as a conductor of that life force, passes it on to those who need help or healing, and thereby healing abilities are made manifest. In my case, I have the ability to act as a conductor of a very high type of energy or life force.

"It is important to realize that there is nothing new on this earth. What happens is that we change the names of various manifestations as we go through various epochs of our civilization in mankind's evolution in human consciousness. Consequently, there is nothing new in what I do. There have been many healers throughout history doing the same thing, although the methods sometimes vary with each individual healer."

Biomagnetic Waves

When asked what she thought took place at a healing session, Mrs B replied: 'The healer unconsciously emits or channels through his or her body, biomagnetic waves. These penetrate the body of the individual, making it possible for the healer to literally feel the disease process of the individual in treatment.

"In my case, it is not at all necessary that I be told that a person has cancer of the throat ... upon making contact with the life force of that individual, I tune in intuitively and know the problem. Physical distress in my body, via the symptom of pain, tells me the location of the disorder. Then, being able to act as a conductor for energy coming from a very high source, I transmit that energy to the individual in accordance with his or her own peculiar need.

This causes not only a change in the apparent condition, but literally a change throughout the entire body of the individual, including a change within his emotional field and a change within his mental field. It is apparent, then, that healing takes place on many different levels. There are isolated manifestations of human life that sometimes cannot be penetrated by this energy, and those cases are what we call 'karmic.' "

Mrs B said she could make such distinctions because of her clairvoyance, which gives her the ability to see the individual in a series of pictures.

She refers to these as "true pictures," and she receives them through concentration. The process, she said, is extremely delicate, and any disturbing factor from the outside could interrupt it.

However, in the healing process, "the transmission of the biomagnetic energy from my body to the individual whom I am treating takes place subconsciously."

Healing, added Mrs B., has been the most dominant thing in her life for almost 50 years.

"I know and have demonstrated that I can transmit the biocurrents into the body of any individual in need, at the best frequency which is most effective and, very importantly, in a manner not the least bit harmful to the living cells.

Cerebral Palsy

"In certain cases, the penetration of this energy into the body is spectacular. For example, when I am treating children who have cerebral palsy, this energy penetrating throughout their energy-exhausted brain cells causes them to 'levitate.'* At my office in Bucharest, I have treated, with fantastic results, children with cerebral palsy, 40 to 50 of them at a time. It was quite spectacular seeing them all levitate simultaneously.

"Since I have come to the United States, I feel my biomagnetic energy has increased. This is especially true in Florida, where I feel that the magnetic radiation of the earth is stronger, and combined with the ultraviolet, electromagnetic irradiation of sunshine and water, has had an increasing effect on strengthening my biomagnetic force."

Mrs B said that her biomagnetic energy also affects vegetables.

"In a recent experiment, I germinated seeds in only a couple of hours that under normal circumstances would have taken several weeks ...

"There are whys and wherefores in the healing process that remain unanswered to me. One thing I know for sure, though; the effect and the result of the treatment depends a great deal on the individual, having a direct bearing on his physical and mental state. It does not, however, depend on whether or not he, himself, believes in the phenomena.

---

* Treating highly sensitive persons, says Mrs B, can sometimes be very spectacular. In both individual or group treatments, the received power sometimes excites the motory muscular system and the commanding nerve centres. When this occurs, one may witness strange, uncontrolled, upward movements of the limbs, head, or the whole body, as if they were weightless. There seems no closer word to describe this process than levitation, and this is the word used by those who have observed such events. Those experiencing this phenomenon are always fully conscious and describe no feelings of discomfort.

"Disregarding the individual's belief or scepticism, this force enters the body, recharges the ill, energy-deprived cells with a new force and improves the circulation. The whole system, mental and physical, is filled with a regenerating life force, and from this stage on, the infirm body is headed towards recovery.

"The basis of a psychic healer's philosophy is that balance must be found between a human system's mental and physical health. The mental and the physical are one. They should be kept in harmony and should be treated as a whole. In my opinion, every disease is curable, but not every individual.

"Let us remember that man is not just his physical body with which he has formerly been identified and with which some are solely identified. He is a number of fields of energy transcending the dense physical, through which that spark of life he calls his individuality or spirit expresses itself.

"It is these fields with which we need to become more familiar. It is these fields we need to research and understand more clearly in order to practically utilize and apply paranormal abilities in our society."

"Finally, it is with purity of motive we need to work ... not for the glamour or sensationalism that can go along with working in parapsychological fields ... not for greed or for the material gain that might be garnered, but with purity of service-oriented attitudes. It is in this spirit that all of us and all of earth's humanity can grow in consciousness and claim our rightful heritage."

Healing in Hungary

Yolanda B was only 18 when she began healing in Hungary. She discovered her powers when something compelled her to lay her hands on the wounded leg of a young boy she encountered one day in a grocery store. The next day his injury reportedly disappeared. A short time later, one of Mrs B's neighbours complained of rheumatism in her arm. When the healer touched her there, she said that she felt an electric shock followed by a sudden relief from pain.

Word spread, and Yolanda became very much in demand, with long waiting lists for her services. From time to time the Communist authorities availed themselves of Mrs B's services and also tolerated the work of scientific institutions that were interested in researching and investigating her powers.

Eventually, however, the growing number of her patients and the 'mystical' nature of the matter made the authorities increasingly uncomfortable with a phenomenon so incompatible with the official materialist-atheist stand. When they became nuisances, Mrs B, heeding the wishes of her family and following an inner drive, came to the United States.

According to Joyce Moore of the Chela Centre, Pompano Beach, Fla., knowledge of Mrs B's gift was widespread throughout Europe. In Hungary, hundreds of people were said to be either temporarily or permanently relieved of actue, chronic, or terminal conditions by virtue of the energy that passed through her body to theirs.

After arriving in the United States, Mrs B said, she was investigated by authorities from several universities and scientific institutions: Dr J.B. Rhine, former professor at Duke University and director of the Foundation for Research on the Nature of Man; and Dr Stanley Dean, professor of psychiatry, University of Miami Medical School and University of Florida Medical School.

Kirlian Photo of Aura

Dr Lyman Fretwell, who does theoretical work in ocean acoustics at the Bell Laboratories in Whippany, N.J., took a Kirlian photograph of Mrs B last year, and was amazed by the strength of her aura.

According to an article in *The New York Times*, Wednesday, June 2, 1976, by Tom Buckley, Dr Fretwell said he'd never seen a picture like hers. "I think she was doing something really powerful here," he said. "After I took it I had to fool with the mechanism for a half-hour before it was working right again, and then the calibrations were entirely different from what they were previously. Yolanda tells me she's always breaking equipment in that way."

Kirlian photography differs from ordinary photography in that the subject places his hand directly on the film, which is enclosed in a lightproof bag. Through some rather complex process, electricity is used to stimulate the aural radiations.

Dr Fretwell, who has a doctorate in physics from the California Institute of Technology, said in the same article:

"I'm simply convinced of the reality of spiritual phenomena. Survival after death, for example. There are many ambiguities. A tremendous amount is unknown. Psychic phenomena is in about the same state physics was in 1600. If you look through the scientific literature of that time, 90 per cent of what was believed was entirely wrong.

"All major discoveries have seemed ambiguous at first. X-rays of crystals, for example, seemed very difficult to interpret, but they proved to lay ʒome of the groundwork for quantum physics."

Dr Robert Vidor, a New Jersey M.D., described Yolanda as "a most remarkable spiritual healer, whose gifts are a blessing to countless suffering people."

It is Mrs B's wish to aid not only the sick, but other healers in developing her kind of therapy. She envisions a clinic of psychic healing, and is especially interested in helping retarded children.

Myoclonic Epilepsy

On the front page of *The Miami Herald*, September 22, 1975, Yolanda B's picture appeared along with an article concerning an afflicted boy whom she reportedly helped. The boy, Mike Flannery, was not able to walk without support because of a rare, inherited disease called myoclonic epilepsy.

The family resorted to Yolanda after years of attempting various kinds of therapy. The article states that after seeing Yolanda, Mike was able to walk alone for the first time in nearly a year, and that his condition had improved.

When Mrs B is challenged by non-believers she replies: "I am not a showman. This power I have, it comes from the one above, who is no fake. The mind of a healer has enormous power; God's power through a channel."

Dr E. Stanton Maxey, a Stuart, Fla., surgeon, told the publication *Super News!* that he refers patients to healers "when my own capacities have been expended to their limits without success."

The article states: "One patient with a breast tumour 'the size of your thumb joint' saw it reduced to 'the size of half a lima bean' after three days of psychic energy treatment by Florida healer Yolanda B. Maxey says he watched the treatment.

" 'Some healers have a special power, a capacity of mind force that causes physical objects to respond to their projected energy, to reorient their biological field,' says Maxey, who has been in practice 18 years and is a board member of the American College of Surgeons.

" 'A state of mind can produce a stomach ulcer or a breast tumour,' he says. 'So if you remedy the state of mind, you may remedy the disease. The human mind obviously plays upon disease. Illness can be induced by our own perceptive capacities. This has been known to medical science for years, yet today we have no understanding of how the human mind works.' "

Dr Robert Vidor of New Jersey, mentioned earlier, set up a series of controlled experiments with Yolanda and worked with her for three weeks. He described her as being "surprisingly accurate in establishing diagnoses."

According to the Florida publication, *The Town Crier*, May 8, 1975, Dr Vidor said: "Almost all patients felt immediately an increase in the sense of well-being and vitality. Instant relief of painful conditions, like arthritis and rheumatism, was frequently observed."

Mrs B has a healing certificate from the Roosevelt Spiritual Memorial Benevolent Association, Miami. She is certified as a teacher and practitioner of parapsychology and has a certificate of appreciation from Miami Dade Community College for service to education as a member of the psycho-bionic symposium. She is also an ordained minister in the American Catholic Church.

According to one of her speeches Yolanda apparently sees herself as a kind of teacher as well as healer: " ... I want to throw some light on the great power of the free will, with its intellectual and moral powers. Only the power of free will can help establish the type of life, the kind of evolution that is the characteristic of every century.

"It is not by choice that we live in our times − that we have our place here and now. It happens because we have a duty to perform by openly talking about our capabilities, and how we are able to make good use of them.

"However, we have to know the ultimate purpose of our being. If we do not know it, we are just as a blind rifleman.

"There are people who are able to further sciences by their supersensitivities. They sense, and come nearer to the unknown. They arrive at that by vitalistic power. They have more insight than the average man. They also know without studying. Some of them are able to sense the other man's inner secrets, his past or even his future. Sometimes it is possible to be incorrect, because of misinterpretation.

"There are individuals who possess more electric magnetism than an average person has in his body. These rare individuals possess radar-like screens in their brains, and so are capable of getting messages, or seeing visions from the past or in the future. Today, everybody is curious about the evolution of things, and the whys. I believe mankind is getting nearer and nearer to discovering the truth.

"Today we have more and more scientists devoting their lives to the discoveries of the power of the mind. We can perfect the long neglected study, and betterment of the mind, so we should be able to discover the true purpose of our being on this planet earth.

"We have perfected fabulous industrial techniques, medical techniques, but the study of the soul has been neglected so far. We should help our scientists of the occult get us out of the terrible mental darkness we live in.

" ... It is a difficult and often thankless job to pull people out of their everyday, routine thinking. Our thinking of today is like a bad tenant who does not pay the rent, and runs away from his responsibility, never to return. If I were not clairvoyant, and a scientist of the occult, I would believe that the soul of mankind has ceased to progress and has been at a standstill for a long, long time."

Meditation

In discussing meditation, Mrs B believes the most difficult part is the ability to clear the brains of all thoughts but one. "If I meditate in this way," she says, "my mental powers grow, my clairvoyant powers clear, and sometimes I am able to perform things you would consider impossible.

"It is possible for all of us to change providing we are the masters of our thoughts and can see our own weaknesses. Then, with humility, we can lift ourselves, along with others, towards betterment of our spiritual life.

" ... We fall, we rise, we fall again, and so on. Finally, we open our eyes. It's not by coincidence that I am here among you. The Lord brought me here with a message. He brought me among a handful of people who possess the sacred feeling of God's nearness that they live up to his teachings and keep his laws. They are not afraid of hardships, nor of being where God wants them to be. This whole globe is a paradise, but too many people want more and more! The thirst for more money obstructs many functions of the brain. There are those to whom sex is of primary importance; they are very poor spiritually.

"Life is so beautiful, in its true sense! It is definitely a perpetual motion leading from birth to death and from death to birth. However, if the soul in its quest attains certain peaks, the earthly ties break, the perpetual motion stops and the soul reaches fantastic heights!

"I know that I was born for a certain purpose, and I do my best to fulfil my mission while I'm among you. I only hope that you feel the necessity and have the courage to learn."

In Hungary, 400 to 500 people reportedly visited Mrs B's clinic in order to receive healing treatments either individually or in mass. One day such healers may be found on the staffs of hospitals in all parts of the world. Perhaps it will eventually be discovered that certain individuals are endowed from birth with the ability to both receive and transmit the energy that heals.

10

THE HEALING ENERGY IN
KUNDALINI AND ANDROGYNY

One of the most mysterious manifestations of the healing energy is the yogic phenomenon known as kundalini. Located at the base of the spine, it generally lies dormant and is frequently visualized as a coiled and sleeping snake, a snake that embodies a particularly potent form of power said to be generated by the mythical goddess, Shakti.

Through a disciplined series of breathing exercises, meditation, and concentration on certain centres of the spine, or chakras, the kundalini may awaken and rise to a site in the brain which is designated as masculine. When this mystical union of the 'female' kundalini with the 'male' component (referred to as Lord Shiva) is achieved, many strange revelations may occur, including what is known as 'enlightenment.'

Most important to our subject, however, is the release of the healing energy, which some people believe to be accomplished through the alchemical or symbolic marriage of feminine and masculine principles, which we may refer to as psychic androgyny.

Meaning of 'Androgynous'
The word androgynous comes from the Greek words *andro*, meaning male, and *gyne*, meaning female. All individuals possess male and female components, and all are, therefore, androgynous. Androgyny in this sense is not to be confused with the physical abnormality known as hermaphroditism, nor with the love and lifestyle associated with bisexuality.

Androgyny here implies the blending of the two complementary psychic forces that are present in all human beings. Theoretically, when these are properly joined, healing occurs through the unity. For example, in acupuncture it is the balanced harmony of the masculine force of *yang* with that of the feminine *yin* that produces health. This concept is apparently a universal one observed throughout antiquity and still evident in various cultures.

As discussed previously, the 'marriage' between the brain's right hemisphere (feminine) and its left (masculine) is presumed to generate health. The high self of the *kahunas* with its powerful healing capacity is usually described as androgynous. And certainly psychiatrist Carl Jung's theories suggest the importance of integrating one's masculine and feminine principles for the sake of mental health.

The healing power unleashed by the kundalini is only one of those associated with androgyny, but it may be the most potent. And those interested in pursuing it should never do so without the guidance of a teacher. For without knowledge of how to control or direct it, this dynamic force can cause serious disorders – physical, mental, and spiritual. Like other varieties of our elusive energy, it can be used to heal, or misused to harm.

Spontaneous Psychic Occurrences

According to some sources, human consciousness is now evolving at such an accelerated rate that some people have begun to experience spontaneous and involuntary psychic occurrences. For instance, individuals who have been meditating regularly for the last several years are now encountering episodes of levitation, psychokinesis, and even dematerialization. Certain spiritual leaders attribute these phenomena to an expanding awareness of the planet. They say it is further evidence that the age of Aquarius is destined to provoke universal enlightenment among humankind. Others ascribe such happenings to the kundalini.

Itzhak Bentov, a Czechoslovakian consultant to industry now living in the United States, believes that the evolution of human consciousness takes place in the nervous system. And in his book, *Stalking the Wild Pendulum*, he suggests that the more highly evolved nervous systems may experience spontaneous and involuntary workings of the kundalini.

In a section called 'The Physio-Kundalini Syndrome,' Bentov writes: 'As has been mentioned before, the human nervous system has a tremendous latent capacity for evolution. This evolution can be accelerated either by meditative techniques, or it may occur spontaneously in an unsuspecting individual. In both cases, a sequence of events is triggered, causing sometimes strong and unusual bodily reactions and unusual psychological states.

"Some of those people who meditate may suspect that these reactions are somehow connected with meditation. Others who develop these symptoms spontaneously may panic and seek medical advice. (Sometimes individuals of both groups may seek medical advice.) Unfortunately, however, Western medicine is presently not equipped to handle these problems. Strangely, in spite of the intensity of the symptoms, little or no physical pathology can be found."

Hindu Life Force

The kundalini is believed to influence the body through a network of 72,000 nadis (nerve channels). The principal nadi is that known as sushumna, which runs inside the spinal column and through the brain to the crown of the head. It is the Hindu life force known as prana, flowing through the sushumna, that is the kundalini. The kundalini is a goddess as well as a snake, and she lies in three and one-half coils in her cave (kanda) at the base of the spine.

The purpose of kundalini yoga is to rouse the sleeping kundalini so that she stretches, hisses, and writhes her way up through the sushumna channel to the top of the head where the Lord Shiva, third god of the Hindu trinity, abides. Shiva represents pure consciousness, and kundalini is a power of the goddess Shakti. The aim of kundalini yoga is accomplished with the union or marriage of Shiva and Shakti.

The Seven Chakras

Prolonged meditation and breathing exercises are essential to awakening the kundalini. The sushumna channel is blocked by the first six or seven major chakras, which are threaded upon it. According to yogi William Zorn in his book, *Yoga for the Mind*, the student intent on making use of the profound mental exercise provided by the actual practice of kundalini yoga should learn all he can about the seven chakras, so that he can find them in introspective exploration, and through his mind's eye visualize the centres in their respective places.

"By unmovingly holding all his mental faculties in the chakras, he will be able to unlock them, thus clearing the way for kundalini. First the muladhara chakra at the lower aperture of the sushumna is opened; once the sea-serpent (or snake) has entered the sushumna of her own accord, she is taken from chakra to chakra as the centres are unlocked. Kundalini continues her upward journey towards her spiritual spouse, the Lord Shiva, residing in the seventh and highest chakra, the sahasrara chakra."

The sahasrara chakra, as described by Zorn, is located at the crown of the head. It is said to shine with the brilliance of many suns; it is the thousand-petalled lotus, the seat of pure consciousness, represented by Shiva.

The muladhara chakra, located at the base of the spinal column between the genital organs and the anus, is represented by a yellow lotus with four crimson petals and is associated with the element earth and the sense of smell.

"Its basic bija, or seed sound," Zorn writes, "is lam. The vowel in lam is kept short and pronounced as in the word 'run.' (The vowels of the bijas of the following four chakras are pronounced the same way.) The last consonant, the 'm,' is continued evenly with the lips closed for as long as the supply of air lasts.

Bija Mantra

"While meditating upon a chakra, the student can, for quicker results, chant its bija, the vibrations of which help to open each particular chakra.

"Situated at the root of the penis," continues Zorn, "is the svadhisthana chakra; this is represented by a white lotus with six vermilion petals. It is allied with the element water and the sense of taste.

"Its bija mantra (seed sound) is vam.

"In the sushumna, at the height of the navel, is the manipura chakra. It is depicted as a red lotus with ten golden petals. It is linked with the element fire and the sense of sight.

"The bija mantra of this chakra is ram.

"The anahata chakra in the region of the heart, is represented by a grey lotus with twelve flaming red petals. The associated element and sense are air and touch, respectively.

"Its bija mantra is yam.

"Situated in the throat region, directly beneath the larynx, the vishuddha chakra is depicted as a white lotus with sixteen purple petals. It is allied with the element ether and the sense of hearing.

"The bija mantra of this chakra is ham.

"The ajna chakra is the command centre, situated midway between the eyebrows. It governs and unifies the faculties represented in the foregoing five chakras. The ajna chakra is the chakra of the mind, and it is represented by a brilliant white lotus with two white petals.

"The bija mantra of the mind centre is Om, and it is this centre that the Yogi recites Om at the time of departure from his physical garb.

"Because of its position in the subcortical area of the brain," writes Zorn, "midway between the eyebrows, and because of the importance of its functions from a yogic point of view, the ajna chakra, or command centre, provides an excellent subject for concentration.

"The student should close his eyes as he brings the full attention of his mind to the point between the eybrows. His concentration will be deep if he unintentionally holds his breath. In the beginning it may help the unruly mind if the closed eyes 'look up' to the spot where the mind is to be focused, but this should not be done to such an extent, and for such a duration, that discomfort is felt.

"Stimulation of this centre through intense and unmoving concentration will give the practitioner greater mental powers.

"As a preliminary exercise to concentration and meditation upon the chakras, yogic breathing is practised. This has the effect of purifying the nadis and paves the way for opening the chakras.

Union with Shiva

"The destination of Shakti (kundalini) is the sahasrara chakra, where union with Shiva takes place – a union symbolic of the joining of man's latent energy with pure consciousness.

"At the finish of the yogi's meditation, Shakti, pregnant with knowledge, retreats to her resting place at the base of the spine. As she goes downward, she vitalizes the chakras, endowing them with consciousness and power. Eventually, the chakras will remain open permanently, leaving a free passage for pure consciousness to flow through."

The reader should be advised, however, that the kundalini should never be awakened without the guidance of a teacher. For without knowledge of how to control or direct it, this mysterious force can cause serious disorders – physical, mental, and spiritual. Like other varieties of the healing energy, it can either kill or cure.

One of the most absorbing properties of the kundalini is its intimation of androgyny. As described earlier, the female kundalini rises to join the male Shiva in a psychic marriage. It is at this point that the individual attains what some people call enlightenment. The kundalini represents one of the female goddesses known as Shakti. Shakti represents the female half of a bisexual primeval entity, the male half being Shiva.

It is Shakti's energy, the kundalini and others, that is responsible for the salvation of individuals. She is sometimes regarded as the dynamic aspect of Brahman, producing the universe through her mysterious power; or a capricious and destructive monarch of nature. Sometimes she is represented as a kindly matriarch; or the ruler of a heavenly court. According to the *Encyclopaedia Britannica*, there is a comprehensive Shaktism that identifies the goddess, usually known as Durga, with Brahman (the supreme being) and worships her as the ruler of the universe; as Mahayogini (Great Mistress of Yoga), she produces, maintains, and reabsorbs the world. As the eternal mother, she is exalted in the Devimahatmya ('glorification of the goddess') section of the *Markandeya-Purana*, an important medieval Shakta encyclopedic text.

In the Bengal cult, Shakti is the evil goddess Kali who demands bloody sacrifices lest her creative potency fail her. The followers of Kali believe birth and death to be inseparable, as are joy and grief, and that all the opposing aspects of the divine should be faced calmly no matter how horrible they might be.

Couplings of Human Beings

In his book, *Yoga for You*, Claude Bragdon suggests that nature's "more obscure and ulterior" purpose for the couplings of human beings is that of higher evolution.

"If man is more than animal, he must have an evolutionary future different from that of the animals. The nature of this evolution, though unguessed by modern materialistic science, has been known from far back by the custodians of the Ancient Wisdom, and by them recorded, but in veiled form, by means of allegory and symbol, to guard these mysteries from profanation and misuse.

Perhaps the nearest approach to a direct statement of the aim and end of human evolution is to be found in the Apocrypha (that part of the Bible rejected by the Reformation): For the Lord Himself, having been asked by someone when His kingdom should come, said, 'When the two shall be one, and the outside as the inside, and the male with the female.'

"This also is in accordance with the *Vedanta* teaching that

Brahman fell asunder into man and wife, and that in the striving of these sundered poles for reunion 'worlds were put forth.' When the two again become one – 'the male with the female' – there ensues the 'night of Brahm,' ending the cycle of manifestation.

"In plain words, it is the ultimate destiny of man to become an androgynous being ... The final phase of sex evolution is the 'divine marriage' of Sol and Luna – that flight of the Alone to the Alone which makes outer and inner one and the same, and puts an end to carnal love by the closing of the 'South Gate,' bringing to birth the beyond-man, or Divine Androgyne: 'For in the resurrection they neither marry nor are given in marriage, but are as the angels of God in Heaven.'"

Androgyny is not Bisexuality

The image of our creator as a divine androgyne is offensive to most followers of the Christian-Judaic faith, which is patriarchal as well as steeped in extreme polarizations of what is feminine and what is masculine. Androgyny, it should be emphasized, is not bisexuality. It is the union of opposing energies, a psychic marriage of what is male and female within us in order to give rebirth to ourselves as more dynamic human beings.

In her book, *Androgyny*, June Singer writes that the kundalini experience brings to consciousness the idea of unity within one's self, a unity of energy and matter, the feminine and the masculine, the physical and the spiritual.

"This path is difficult," she writes, "arduous and demanding, but kundalini yoga offers one possibility for achieving one's androgynous potential. It requires a rigidly ascetic discipline; it leads its adherents to the experience of our temporal world as illusory and of little value in comparison with the attainment of non-dual awareness of the 'Undivided Whole,' the non-separability of the created and the Increate."

Dr Singer also suggests that the Judaic-Christian deity, long considered male, may Himself have been androgynous, and she speculates as to whether biblical translators may not have concealed this information.

Elohim

As an example, the Hebrew word for God as used through the Old

Testament is Elohim: "In the beginning Elohim created the heavens and the earth." Interestingly enough, Elohim is the plural form of the feminine word, Eloh or Eloha.

According to S.L. MacGregor Mathers, in his introduction to *The Kabbalah Unveiled*, the interpreters of the Bible, hoping to eradicate any allusion to the notion of an androgynous deity, translated a feminine plural by a masculine singular in the case of the word, Elohim. "They have, however," writes Mathers, "left an inadvertent admission of their knowledge that it was plural in Gen. iv. 26; 'And Elohim said: Let Us make man.' Again (v.27), how could Adam be made in the image of Elohim, male and female, unless the Elohim were male and female also? The word Elohim is a plural-formed from the feminine singular, ALH, Eloh, by adding IM to the word. But inasmuch as IM is usually the termination of the masculine plural, and is here added to a feminine noun, it gives to the word Elohim the sense of a female potency united to a masculine idea, and thereby capable of producing an offspring.

"Now, we hear much of the Father and the Son, but we hear nothing of the Mother in the ordinary religions of the day. But in the Qabalah we find that the Ancient of Days conforms Himself simultaneously into the Father and the Mother, and thus begets the Son. Now, this Mother is Elohim.

"Again, we are usually told that the Holy Spirit is masculine. But the word RVCH, *Ruach*, Spirit, is feminine, as appears from the following passage ... 'Achath *(feminine not Achad, masculine) Ruach Elohim Chiim*: One is *She* the Spirit of the Elohim of Life.' Now, we find that before the Deity conformed Himself thus – i.e., as male and female – that the worlds of the universe could not subsist, or, in the words of Genesis, 'The earth was formless and void.'"

And, again, what has adrogyny got to do with the healing energy? A great deal. In acupuncture, as previously noted, the rebalancing of the *yin* (female) and the *yang* (male) is presumably what restores health. In fact, balanced interplay between an individual's male and female components as a necessity to well-being has been a consistent, almost universal theme throughout history.

Dr Irving Oyle, in *The Healing Mind*, writes: "Ease, as opposed to disease, may be seen as a state of harmonious equilibrium between the two equipotent, autonomous, cerebral hemispheres, one of which is conscious (sun, yang, male), and one of which is subconscious (moon, yin, female). If contact is established between the two hemispheres (the alchemical mystical marriage), healing energy (the panacea) is released. The healing energy is the same as the energy tied up in the symptom (the *prima materia*)."

'The Woman Within'

In *Man and His Symbols*, Carl Jung writes: "In the Middle Ages, long before the physiologists demonstrated that by reason of our glandular structure there are both male and female elements in all of us, it was said that 'every man carries a woman within himself.' It is this female element in every male that I have called the 'anima.' This 'feminine' aspect ... is kept carefully concealed from others as well as from oneself. In other words, though an individual's visible personality may seem quite normal, he may well be concealing from others – or even from himself – the deplorable condition of 'the woman within.'"

Jung referred to the "inner man" within a woman's psyche as the animus. In the following, he supports the premise of the brain's right hemisphere, which controls the left side of the body, as being masculine and the left, which controls the right side of the body, as being feminine:

"A woman patient who had unfulfilled longings for a career, which she had had to give up for a very difficult and short-lived marriage, dreamed that she was kneeling opposite a man who was also kneeling. He had a ring that he prepared to put on her finger, but she stretched out her right-hand ring finger in a tense manner – evidently resisting this ritual of marital union.

"It was easy to point out her significant error. Instead of offering the left-hand ring finger (by which she could accept a balanced and natural relation to the masculine principle) she had wrongly assumed that she had to put her entire conscious (i.e., right-sided) identity in the service of the man.

In fact, marriage required her to share with him only that subliminal, natural (i.e., left-sided) part of herself in which the principle of union would have a symbolic, not a literal or absolute meaning. Her fear was the fear of the woman who dreads to lose her identity in a strongly patriarchal marriage, which this woman had good reason to resist."

Dogon Myth

The androgyne, as a symbol of holistic perfection, plays a part in the creation myths of numerous cultures. A good example is an African myth from the Dogon peoples of West Africa. In this myth the androgynous deity first creates an egg. "Within the egg," according to the *Encyclopaedia Britannica*, "are two pairs of twins, each pair consisting of one male and one female. These twins are supposed to mature within the egg, becoming at maturation androgynous (both male and female) beings, the perfect creatures to inhabit the earth.

One of the twins breaks from the egg before maturation because he wishes to dominate the creation. In so doing, he carries a part of the egg with him, and from this he creates an imperfect world. The creator deity, seeing what he has done, sacrifices the other twin to establish a balance in the world."

Socrates's Discourse on Love

Androgyny was recorded in ancient Greece through the pen of Plato in his *Symposium*. The following, abridged from the translation of W.H.D. Rouse in *Great Dialogues of Plato*, is a part of Socrates's discourse on love and its infinite variety:

"Formerly, the natural state of man was not what it is now, but quite different. For at first there were three sexes, not two as at present, male and female, but also a third having both together; the name (androgynes) remains with us, but the thing is gone. There was then a male-female sex and a name to match (the word androgynous means sharing both male and female) ..., but now nothing is left but the title used in reproach.

"Next, the shape of (each being of all three sexes) was quite round, back and ribs passing about it in a circle; and (each individual) had four arms and an equal number of legs, and two faces on a round neck, exactly alike; there was one head with these two opposite faces, and four ears, and two privy members, and the rest as you might imagine from this. They walked upright as now, in whichever direction they liked; and when they wanted to run fast, they rolled over and over on the ends of the eight limbs ... with their legs straight out. And why there were three sexes, and shaped like this, was because the male was at first born of the sun, and the female of the earth, and the common sex had something of the moon, which combines both male and female; their shape was round and their going was round because they were like their parents. They had terrible strength and force, and great were their ambitions; they attacked the gods, and ... they tried to climb into heaven ...

"So Zeus and the other gods held council what they should do, and they were perplexed; for they really could not kill the tribe with thunderbolts and make them vanish like the giants ... nor could they allow them to go on in this wild way.

"After a deal of worry Zeus had a happy thought. 'Look here,' he said, 'I think I have found a scheme; we can let men still exist but we can stop them from their violence by making them weaker ... I will slice each of them down through the middle! Two improvements at once! They will be weaker, and they will be more useful to us because there will be more of them. They shall walk upright on two legs ... and then he sliced (them) through the middle ... as you slice hard-boiled eggs with a hair ...

"So when the original body was cut through, each half wanted the other, and hugged it; they threw their arms round each other desiring to grow together in the embrace, and died of starvation and general idleness because they would not do anything apart from each other. When one of the halves died and the other was left, the half which was left hunted for another and embraced it ...

"Unfortunately, they rarely found their true and proper other half; as a result, they began to perish.

"But Zeus pitied them and found another scheme; he moved their privy part in front, for these also were outside before, and they had begotten and brought forth not with each other but with the ground, like the cicadas. So he moved these parts also in front and made the generation come between them, by the male in the female; that in this embrace, if a man met a woman, they might beget and the race might continue, and if a man met a man, they might be satisfied by their union and rest, and might turn to work and care about the general business of life. So you see how ancient is the mutual love implanted in mankind, bringing together the parts of the original body, and trying to make one out of two, and to heal the natural structure of man.

"Then each of us is the tally (half) of a (human being); sliced like a flatfish. So each one seeks his other tally."

Here Plato explains that all those who were originally individuals of the androgynous beings seek their other halves in a heterosexual fashion, the man after his woman and the woman after her man. But "the women who are a cutting of the ancient women (both halves female) do not care much about men, but are more attracted to women ..." And those men who are a cutting of the ancient men (both halves male) also seek their own kind.

"So when one of these meets his own proper half (male or female) they are wonderfully overwhelmed by affection and intimacy and love, and one may say, never wish to be apart for a moment." All of love, continues Plato, is simply the pursuit and desire for the wholeness that was once our natural shape.

Hermes Trismegistus

Although Plato may have used androgyny as a legendary explanation for heterosexuality in the above, he was undoubtedly influenced by writings attributed to the legendary Egyptian sage, Hermes Trismegistus. This fabled teacher, who became deified as a god of wisdom, is reported to have said in ancient documents that the original creator (God) was both male and female, the divine androgyne who made the first human beings in his own image. After a long period, for the sake of population growth, the androgynes were "loosed apart," some becoming male and some female.

Some believe that Western culture would be greatly improved if the creator were to be considered androgynous rather than strictly or merely male. And perhaps the notion would appease those who advocate a return to goddess worship or matriarchy as the only possible course. For example, Elizabeth Gould Davis advises us in her feisty work, *The First Sex*:

"The rot of masculist materialism has indeed permeated all spheres of twentieth-century life and now attacks its very core. The only remedy for the invading and consuming rot is a return to the values of the matriarchates, and the rediscovery of the non-material universe that had so humanizing an influence on the awakening minds of our ancestors.

"Physicists of many nations are today gaining a new understanding of this invisible world as they discover almost daily some new phenomenon of nature that cannot be explained by our accepted laws of physics. There is, apparently, a physics of the *supernatural* whose laws modern man has been totally unaware of and to which he is only now becoming attuned.

"It was the knowledge of this other world, possessed by the women of old and utterly discredited by later materialistic man, that gave early woman her power over man."

Mental and Spiritual Gifts

"In the new science of the twenty-first century, not physical force but spiritual force will lead the way. Mental and spiritual gifts will be more in demand than gifts of a physical nature. Extrasensory perception will take precedence over sensory perception. And in this sphere woman will again predominate. She who was revered and worshipped by early man because of her power to see the unseen will once again by the pivot – not as sex but as divine woman – about whom the next civilization will, as of old, revolve."

The loss of the female principle in religion was lamented, as a matter of fact, as long ago as 800 B.C. by the Greek poet Hesiod, who wrote:

"During the golden and silver ages of goddess-rule, men lived without cares, never growing old or weary, dancing and laughing much; death to them was no more terrible than sleep."

The ancient concept of a divine androgyne contains and combines the male and female components that exist throughout nature. There are some who postulate that the revival of such personified harmony would do much to improve the human race.

It might also, along with proper control of the kundalini, help us to understand the complex nature of the energy that heals.

11

THE HEALING ENERGY IN NEW-AGE THERAPIES

Acupuncture

One of the most persuasive arguments for healing energy theories is the acknowledged success of acupuncture. The energy employed in this ancient art is known as *ch'i*, which has already been discussed in several sections of this book.

Traditional acupuncture is a healing science that originated in China about 5000 years ago. A highly intricate and complex system of examination, diagnosis, and treatment, acupuncture studies the entire human being: his body, mind, and spirit. Most of us in the West are aware of acupuncture's use as an anaesthetic. But this, in actuality, is only one part of what this discipline is all about.

Although acupuncture is preventive in the sense of maintaining and creating health, it also recognizes the process of illness and offers the means of restoring normalcy.

According to Dr Dianne M. Connelly, in her book, *Traditional Acupuncture: The Law of the Five Elements,* "the main difference between Western medicine and Oriental medicine is the basic theory of the Chinese that there is a life force called *ch'i* energy, and that this life force flows within us in a harmonious, balanced way. This harmony and balance is health. If the life force is not flowing properly, then there is disharmony and imbalance. This is illness."

Like homoeopaths, acupuncturists study not only the symptoms of disease but the whole person. Each patient is analyzed according to the sound of his voice, the colour and texture of his skin, the predominant emotion, the posture and carriage, favourite foods, sleeping habits, the best and worst times of the day, sexual energy, intestinal and bladder function, stresses, interests, and other particulars in order to make an accurate diagnosis of his illness.

Pulse Diagnosis

According to Dr Connelly, one of the most important tools in this process is pulse diagnosis. "The pulses are the reading of the state of energy in the bodymind. Each of the other correspondences tell us either a little bit about the energy or what element to look at as the one being most in need of balancing, but it is the pulses which focus all this information.

"Each organ is associated with a pulse and other facets of life: an emotion, a taste, a colour, a time of day, a season, an odour, a sound, a sense organ, a body orifice, a pathway where the ch'i energy flows and so forth ...

"In a very cursory way this means that a person who has an imbalance in the flow of the ch'i energy that controls the kidneys may also be exhibiting related symptoms such as a craving for salt, an excess of fear, a preference for or intense dislike of the colour blue, a lack of will power, ear troubles, an abhorrence of cold weather, sexual inadequacy or pains along the specific pathway of energy that governs the kidneys. Each organ has its correlations. Two people may have the same or similar symptoms, yet the diagnosis and treatment vary extensively."

The pathways in the body along which the ch'i energy flows are called meridians. In order to remove blockage along these meridian pathways (or lines), the acupuncturist, at specific points along them, inserts needles of pure copper, gold, or silver. The needles, which are slipped in just below the skin, generate a current of impulse along the meridian line. Acting upon the central nervous system, this impulse affects the corresponding organ that is out of balance.

In other words, the ch'i, which flows along the meridians, is circulated through the entire body. It controls the circulation of blood, ingestion, and the immunizing system of the body. When for some reason it becomes blocked, an abnormal excess or paucity of energy results. This situation is remedied by either a stimulating or sedating treatment at the proper acupuncture points.

Yin and Yang

The ch'i energy manifests itself through two polar forces: the yin (feminine) and the *yang* (masculine). According to *The Chinese Art of Healing,* by Stephan Palos, good or bad health is determined by the fluctuations of these conflicting forces. There is a constant struggle in the human organism, as in nature, between these opposing principles.

"Originally *yin* signified the northern and *yang* the southern side of a mountain on which the sun shone. *Yin* terms included negation, cold, dark, and female, whereas *yang* personified positive, male, light, and warmth. Just as these two forces are in constant conflict in the universe and yet at the same time form a whole, so too do they symbolize harmony or disharmony in the human organism.

"An evenly balanced, equipoised *yin* and *yang* means good health – but if the energy is displaced in any one direction it denotes illness. Over-powerful *yang* symbolizes increased organic activity; if, on the other hand, *yin* predominates, this implies hypofunction.

"Just as the continuous interplay of these two opposing forces produces all phenomena in the universe – as, for example, the changing seasons and the sequence of night and day – so too does it produce in the human organism the inhalation and exhalation of air and the conditions of waking and sleeping. The *yin-yang* principle also accounts for parallels between sympathetic and parasympathetic nervous systems."

The idea of androgyny comes to mind whenever the unity of these two polar forces is stressed, and, of course, the healing energy seems to manifest itself when the two components are at ease rather than in a state of disease.

The Five Elements

Closely related to the *yin-yang* principle is the doctrine of the five elements, which are wood, fire, earth, metal, and water. According to Stephan Palos, they can exist in a helpful and complementary relationship to each other or work against one another to destroy themselves.

"The doctrine of the elements," Palos writes, "no doubt has its origins in very ancient concepts. It is perhaps possible to read into it such a context as: fire is fed by wood; after the fire has burned itself out there remain ashes which become earth, in which metals are found and from which water springs; the water feeds the trees, thus completing the circle back to the element of wood.

"Such a sequence is, in part, supported by the traditional art of healing," Palos writes. "But in another respect the elements are in opposition to one another: the antipole of fire is metal; the antipole of earth is water. Metal and wood cancel each other out, as do water and fire, or wood and earth ..."

The *yin-yang* principle and the five elements are considered by the Chinese to control all of nature as well as man and illustrate how the two coincide. Nature is the macrocosm, man the microcosm. Or, as above, so below.

Unique Feature of Acupuncture

In *A Guide to Alternative Medicine*, Donald Law writes: "There is a unique feature of acupuncture which I must describe. When a patient has the needles inserted correctly he can calmly watch the surgeons cut away part of his stomach during an operation, and a woman may watch her child being born. This is because acupuncture obviates the need for any anesthetics.

"There are no noxious potions, nothing to upset the patient, and since no messages of pain have been tearing down to the brain from an outraged nervous system, there are no after-effects at all. The patient just begins to feel better. Some have been known to eat fruit during an operation on the spine!

"Acupuncture is one of the most amazing branches of healing. In case anybody doubts the existence of the meridians, I am informed that the Chinese have managed to prove their existence both by electronic aids and by a specialized form of photography."

Mr Law also mentions an article written by Winston Churchill, M.P., in the *London Observer*, April 30, 1972, that describes the removal of brain tumours and thyroid, correction of pressure by spinal vertebra on spinal-cord nerves, gastric operations and several deaf-mute cures, all solely by acupuncture.

Sometimes acupuncture produces unexpected side benefits. One woman I spoke with. said she had received treatment for a general ailment and suddenly found the sight of one eye had been restored. And a young man, without dieting, unaccountably lost 20 unwanted pounds. He was convinced that the weight loss was due to the rebalancing of his feminine and masculine principles (the *yin* and the *yang*).

Acupuncture represents the ancient art of Chinese healing in its most complete and systematic form. There are other Oriental disciplines, however, that are based on the same tenets.

T'ai-Chi

T'ai-chi or *t'ai-chi-ch'uan* is another Chinese discipline that operates on the theory of *ch'i* energy. Developed originally as a martial art, it is a system of slow, carefully ordered exercises that are said to keep the body's energies in balance. The motions are performed loosely and flexibly; their purpose is control of the body through inward calm.

Again, we see the attempt to produce equilibrium through the balancing of *yin* and *yang* in order to prevent illness. In fact, morning and evening sessions of *t'ai-chi* are considered an easy form of preventive medicine. The exercises are easy and involve normal breathing at all times. The *t'ai-chi* practitioner thinks of his bones as a series of small 'cylinders' linked together by loose joints and supported by the spinal column. The aim is to keep the 'cylinders' in a state of stability. The basic principles of *t'ai-chi*, as well as other Oriental exercises, have been outlined in the previously quoted book, *The Chinese Art of Healing*, by Stephan Palos:

"1. The exercises require no effort. Permanent co-ordination of all the limbs is achieved by concentration alone. If the movements are angular, they must be rounded off; if they are unco-ordinated, they must be co-ordinated. Every part of the body must be maintained in a loose and relaxed state.

"2. Every movement starts from the sacral area. The 'sacrum' must remain 'quiet and firm.' Thus Chinese authors employ a metaphor according to which the sacrum is the main shaft while the extremities are the small ones; or, if the sacrum is the large 'cylinder,' then the extremities are the small ones.

"3. Every movement is carried out in a circular direction. Although arms and legs appear to move 'angularly' in their sockets, in actual fact they describe either circles or semicircles in their swivel joints. In older times this was expressed by saying that every square contains a circle, and vice versa.

"4. Equilibrium must be obtained during every phase of movement. This can be done by constantly striving to have a prepared centre of gravity which will suit both the defence and attack positions.

"5. Physiotherapeutic movements must be smooth and uninterrupted, like slow-motion pictures. The Chinese compare them to the movements of cattle chewing the cud.

"6. Large weights can be moved with little expenditure of energy. The body must therefore not be tensed; on the contrary, the idea is to carry out the exercises with a continuous 'momentum' and maintain the equilibrium in harmony with the constantly changing centre of gravity.

"7. 'Strength' and 'lack of strength' must be shared, which means that excess weight develops on the side of which the exerciser is leaning, and that this excess must be balanced by the 'vacuum' on the other side.

"8. 'Upper' and 'Lower' must follow one another, which means that the arms and legs must be moved alternately.

"9. Breathing must be deep and quiet. The shoulders must also be kept still, otherwise the person doing the exercises will begin to gasp.

"10. 'Movement must be peaceful and all peace contains movement.' This is an alternative way of expressing the yin-yang principle and denotes 'passivity in activity' and 'activity in passivity.' It thus follows that all movements should be reflex controlled."

The Chinese believe that the essence of the exercises, with their requisites of stamina, concentration, continuity, and gradual intensification is of spiritual nature.

According to Palos:

"Exercises are normally carried out in the open air, if possible in a sheltered position. The best times have proved to be half an hour before going to bed and half an hour after getting up. No heavy meals should be taken immediately before or after the exercises, and the same applies to drinking and smoking. No impeding clothing should be worn.

108 Movement Phases

"The complete series of exercises comprises some 108 movement phases, the precise number varying from author to author. During all phases the arms, legs, and head are moved in various directions with a circular motion. Old books on the subject even attached significance to the different points of the compass, but this may be disregarded. The exercises can be carried out alone or in pairs. In the latter case, two persons stand facing one another and carry out either identical or complementary movements.

Thus the various forms of attack and defence are run through in the slow motion, as it were. Whenever one of the participants puts his left foot forward, his opposite number likewise takes a step forward with his left foot; or, if the one partner lowers his arms, the other rotates his raised arms, so that together they form a unified motion. The exercises last approximately 20 to 25 minutes.

"There is also an 'advanced school' of gymnastic exercises wherein physical and mental equilibrium are combined on a higher plane. This special series of exercises is called *Ta Lu* ('the great repulse'). This means that in cases both of actual attack or its simulation, the actor not only repels the attacker by physical force alone – he also increases the power of his bodily strength by means of the energy generated by his 'calm spirit' and his steady concentration."

Renewal Vitality and Longevity

According to the Chinese the practice of *t'ai-chi* for 20 minutes a day is very rejuvenating. Every part of the body is used during the exercises and stimulated by the flowing movement. Renewed vitality and longevity are said to reward the consistent practitioner. *Ch'uan* means fist, and *t'ai-chi-ch'uan* a martial art of fisticuffs, attempts to ward off the most difficult of all adversaries, death.

Through the ritual of the exercises, the *ch'i* force is said to be accumulated and stored in a small area of the lower abdomen. Once captured, it is believed that the *ch'i* can be circulated throughout the body as instructed by the mind.

Mark Bricklin, editor of *Prevention,* in his book, *The Practical Encyclopedia of Natural Healing,* quotes an ancient Chinese treatise on *t'ai-chi*: "The mind directs the *ch'i,* which sinks deeply and permeates the bones. The *ch'i* circulates freely, mobilizing the body so that it needs the direction of the mind. If the *ch'i* is correctly cultivated, your spirit of vitality will rise and you will feel as though your head were suspended by a string from above."

Bricklin also quotes the late Master William C.C. Chen of the T'ai-Chi School in New York as saying of *ch'i*: "It is certainly a mystery, but it works. Look at acupuncture; it has cured apparently incurable diseases, even though it is not yet clear how it works. All I can say is, if you practice *T'ai-Chi* every day, you will eventually build up this inner strength or *ch'i*."

Master Chen once demonstrated the power of *ch'i* in Madison Square Garden's Forum. A motor cycle carrying four strong young men rode over his stomach as he lay on the floor. He remained unaffected and was still smiling even after the motor cyclists took turns punching him in the abdomen. When one considers that Chen, at the time, was old, very short (under five feet), and tiny-boned, the feat seems all the more remarkable.

Acupressure

Acupressure is probably best described as acupuncture in massage form, or a cross between the two. Instead of using needles, acupressure involves the massaging of points along the 12 meridians in order to rebalance the *ch'i* energy. The practice is said to be older than acupuncture – as ancient, in fact, as touch itself.

One fairly well-known form of therapy that utilizes acupressure, as well as judo, spinal correction, and exercise, is *shiatsu*, also called Japanese finger pressure massage. Here, finger pressure, especially the thumb, is used to depress or stimulate the flow of *ch'i* (called *ki* in Japan).

George Downing, in *The Massage Book,* believes *shiatsu* is quite easily learned. "Pressure," he writes, "is applied with the thumbs for several seconds at a time to any or all of hundreds of points located throughout the body. A complete massage usually covers every part of the body; when done for medical purposes, however, only certain combinations of points may be brought into play.

"*Shiatsu* is tiring to do at first because of the sustained use of the thumbs. Even a tiny bit practised each day, however, quickly gives the thumbs the necessary strength and endurance.

"Besides being an interesting form of massage in its own right, *shiatsu* can serve as an extremely effective change of pace when combined with Western forms of massage. It also can be used for self-massage, since many of the points it makes use of can be massaged by a person himself."

Another reason daily self-massage is beneficial: according to *shiatsu* theory, the fingers are closely related to key organs of the body, while the entire left hand is connected to the heart. This type of self-massage, therefore, may serve to strengthen the entire body.

Relieving a Sore Throat

Developed about 40 years ago by Tokujiro Namikoshi in Japan, *shiatsu* is now experiencing unexpected popularity in the United States. In *The Practical Encyclopedia of Natural Healing* quoted previously, Mark Bricklin suggests: "If you want to give *shiatsu* a try, a good time to do so would be when you have a cold or the flu, accompanied by a sore throat, fever, and perhaps diarrhoea. To reduce the pain of sore throat by *shiatsu* principles, grasp your left thumb with your right hand. At the bottom corner of the U around the thumbnail, on the side facing towards your body, there is a point located a scant one-tenth of an inch in from the corner.

Instead of using the pressure of the bulb of your thumb, place the thumbnail of your right hand directly over the target point on your left thumb and press vigorously. Hold the pressure about seven seconds and then release it. There should be a mark in your skin when you release the pressure. Repeat three times. Then switch hands and apply pressure to the inside corner of your right-hand thumb with your left thumbnail.

Relieving Fever and Diarrhoea

"To relieve fever and diarrhoea according to *shiatsu* techniques, move to the index finger. Here, locate the same point you are using on your thumb, which you will find just a tiny fraction of an inch from the corner of the nail, on the side facing your thumb. Again, use the thumbnail of the opposite hand and apply pressure for five to seven seconds, repeating three times on both hands."

Shiatsu is also said to be remarkably effective in treating sexual problems and in increasing potency.

A less familiar form of acupressure is that known as *jin shin jyutsu.* Like acupuncture, this therapy is based upon the flow of *ch'i* or *ki* throughout the body, and it involves all of the standard acupuncture meridians. According to a recent article in *East West Journal* called 'Jin Shin Jyutsu,' by Ron and Iona Teeguarden, the practice was instituted by the Japanese master, Jiro Murai, who had devoted his lifetime to the research of both acupressure and acupuncture.

Like most acupressure systems, *jin shin*, which may be translated as the art of circulation awakening, is based upon a selected number of acupuncture points. Master Jiro Murai chose the 30 major bilateral ones because he felt it was at these spots that blockages in the energy flow were most likely to occur.

"Since these blocks either manifest as or are caused by physical tension, *jin shin jyutsu* works to both release the muscular tensions and to redirect and balance the energy flows. On a physical level, the *jin shin* pressure method breaks down the adhering fascial tissues (sheaths of connective tissue which can grow over and bind together a group of muscles which should be working separately) and releases the accumulated fatigue toxins (by-products of muscle work).

"Since these toxins are known to be major causes of fatigue, a common result of a *jin shin jyutsu* treatment is, first, deep sleep during and after the treatment and, next, renewed energy and strength the next day – as well as a feeling of lightness and relief from tension and anxiety ... As the energy flows are released, redirected, stimulated, and balanced, these flows are able to effectively continue their function of directing the body's activities.

"This is why a *jin shin jyutsu* treatment is said to not only last an hour – the average treatment time – but in effect to last two hours. For in this space of time, *ch'i* ascends and descends consecutively through all of the major meridians, and the newly balanced and strengthened flow has its effect on each meridian in turn. So the release goes deeper."

Reflexology

Reflexology, also known as zone therapy, has been used by the Chinese for 5000 years. According to George Downing in *The Massage Book*, the principle behind this technique is simple: "For every important organ or muscle area in the trunk and head there is a tiny area that corresponds to it on one or both feet. To locate and treat a health problem affecting any of the upper part of the body you merely massage the corresponding area on the foot."

Admitting that the premise sounds bizarre, Downing continues: "I can only say that I have been experimenting with zone therapy on an informal basis for some time, as have a number of others with whom I am in contact, and I am convinced that there is a great deal to it. It is not a cure-all, and it is definitely no substitute for a visit to the doctor's office. But as a supplement to ordinary medical attention it can often provide a small but noticeable boost in health wherever it is needed.

"Why does it work? There are a lot of theories. One frequently advanced is that it is the nervous system which is responsible: numerous nerves running from the foot to elsewhere in the body can cause a reflex action in any other appropriate body part, and this in turn, by stimulating circulation, can bring about a better nutritional intake and elimination of waste in the immediate neighbourhood of that same part.

Another hypothesis – and my own suspicions are that the truth lies more in this direction – is that the connective tissue and the lymph system throughout the body are the vehicles for energy circuits of a nature as yet unanalyzed by medical science, and that the right kind of massage work on the foot unblocks an energy flow that also affects the corresponding area of the body."

Crystalline Deposits

Dr Maybelle Segal in her book, *Reflexology,* describes the therapy as "a natural and drugless way of stimulating the internal organs and increasing circulation to all areas. It is based on the theory that if the body is in a healthy condition, with no congestion in it, no tender areas should be found on the feet. However, if any part of the body is not functioning properly, it will be manifested by tender areas in the feet. This tenderness is caused by crystalline deposits which form at the nerve endings in the feet. They may be acid or alkaline in character, but they do denote congested areas in the body, and this congestion interferes with the circulation in the body ... Deposits must be worked out in order to improve the circulation of the body.

"At times a person massaging the feet may actually feel the deposits (depending on the size of them). While at other times the deposits may feel like gravel (but are no less painful). At still other times no deposits may be felt, but the person being massaged will let you know very clearly that the tenderness *is* there.

"The purpose in doing compression foot massage is to break up these deposits (or crush them) so that they may become solvent and be carried away with the rest of the waste material in the body. Once these deposits are dissolved, the congestion is relieved, and the circulation to the body is improved. Since the body works as a unit, the malfunctioning of even one part of the body will affect the rest of it."

Reflexology is useful in diagnosis as well as in therapy. Any spot that seems unduly sensitive when pressed may indicate a need for treatment in the corresponding organ.

My own experience with reflexology has been quite successful. The practitioner, a registered nurse and professional masseuse, believes that reflexology increases the flow of nerve energy and keeps the body attuned through circulation. She also compares the process to acupressure, and often senses a flow of energy being transmitted between herself and patients.

Fortunately, since it is difficult to massage one's own feet, the hands also have reflex areas that respond to the various organs of the body.

By massaging and applying firm pressure to the upper part of one's thumbs, for instance, reflexologists say that it is possible to gain quick relief from headaches.

Reichian Therapeutics

The basic theory behind Reichian therapeutics is that all emotional problems reveal themselves unconsciously in the body. Depression, rage, and the inability to love produce physical reactions; Reichian therapists, therefore, work through the patient's body to achieve mental health.

Orgone therapy, as mentioned in Chapter 8, involved the breaking down of patient's armouring as it existed in his muscles, thus allowing the free flow of orgone energy throughout the body. A good description of this process occurs in Orson Bean's *Me and the Orgone*:

"Reich's treatment consisted, in a nutshell, of breaking down the armouring and thereby restoring the natural self-regulative process. Using his physician's knowledge of musculature, he discovered exactly which muscles controlled which functions. He found that by kneading, pressing or jabbing at certain muscles used to inhibit crying, he could make the patient spontaneously start to sob, and he found that other muscles, when jabbed at or pressed, would cause rage-filled screaming. He encouraged his patients to give in to these natural functions.

"At first, the patients felt embarrassed to rant and rave and sob but in a short time they felt overwhelming relief at being able to express their feelings fully. Reich discovered that as his patients found themselves able to cry and rage again, the old feelings from the days when they originally armoured themselves came to the surface and could be analyzed. The armouring, it seemed, was not symptomatic of neurosis but was, in fact, the actual physical counterpart of the neurosis. As it was broken down, vivid dreams occurred which the patient was often spontaneously able to analyze himself.

"Reich found that in his armoured patients breathing was shallow, and he worked with them to get them to breathe more freely and deeply. The holding in of the chest and diminishing of the breathing function was in itself, it turned out, a defence mechanism against feelings in the area. When this defence was broken down, all kinds of deep feelings flooded out, which under classical psychiatry would have taken years to reach, if they could be reached at all.

Freedom from Internal Bondage

"Reich discovered that it was very important for a doctor to learn in what order the armouring should be broken down (eyes and mouth first, chest second, etc.). He also learned that the very thing the patient wanted, freedom from his internal bondage, was what terrified him most.

"As each new area of armouring was broken down, the patient would feel elated at first and then absolutely terrified. It was as though the armouring had become part of the personality and as *it* went, he felt that *he* was going. Patients told him they literally felt they were going to die, that they were coming apart, that they had nothing to hold onto. All Reich could do was counsel them to tolerate the fear and tell themselves that they weren't going to die. Those who were able to stick it out found themselves changing profoundly."

Because of the emphasis on sex in Wilhelm Reich's theories, it was often erroneously assumed that the same emphasis existed in his applied therapeutics. According to those who knew Reich, and especially those who were in therapy with him, such assumptions were totally unrelated to the truth.

Dr Alexander Lowen, a neo-Reichian psychiatrist, describes his therapy with Reich in the book *Bioenergetics*:

"During his work with me Reich occasionally applied pressure with his hands to some of the tense muscles in my body to help them relax. Usually, with me and with others, he applied such pressure to the jaw. In most people the jaw muscles are extremely tense – the jaw held tightly in an attitude of determination often verging on grimness or thrust forward defiantly or abnormally retracted.

"In all these cases the jaw is not fully mobile, and its fixed position denotes a structured attitude. Under pressure jaw muscles become tired and 'let go.' As a result, the breathing becomes freer and deeper, and often involuntary tremours occur in the body and the legs.

"Other areas of muscular tension to which pressure was applied were the back of the neck, the lower back and the adductor muscles of the thighs. In all cases pressure was applied selectively only to those areas in which chronic muscular spasticity could be palpated."

Bioenergetics

It was Dr Lowen who developed the now well-known neo-Reichian therapy called bioenergetics. The system is based on the principle that the human body is an energy system, and that its energy must flow freely if health is to be maintained.

This free flow is accomplished by unlocking physical tensions and unleashing dammed-up emotions. In practice, this system combines a variety of treatments, including exercise, deep breathing, conventional psychoanalysis, and certain forms of Gestalt psychotherapy.

In *Bioenergetics*, Lowen writes: "Bioenergetics is a therapeutic technique to help a person get back together with his body and to help him enjoy to the fullest degree possible the life of the body. This emphasis on the body includes sexuality, which is one of its basic functions. But it also includes the even more basic functions of breathing, moving, feeling and self-expression.

"A person who doesn't breathe deeply reduces the life of his body. If he doesn't feel fully, he narrows the life of his body. And if his self-expression is constricted, he limits the life of his body."

Today, there are many therapies that attempt to reach the emotions through the body. Structural integration, better known as Rolfing because it was developed by Ida Rolf; patterning, developed by Judith Aston in collaboration with Dr Rolf; the Alexander technique by F. Matthias Alexander; and the Feldenkrais method by Moshe Feldenkrais are probably the most notable examples. But when Reich instituted orgone therapy, the very idea of physical contact, no matter how slight, was considered taboo.

It is difficult in this era of freedom to realize what a giant step Reich took when he decided that the unconscious could be made conscious through the body, that repressed hostility could be unlocked through the muscles, that memories long thought dead can be revived through the skin. All those who have been helped by therapies that reach emotional substance through physical form are at least partially in debt to Wilhelm Reich.

Transcendental Meditation

Transcendental meditation is a technique that can be learned in four two-hour classes. Students receive a secret word or mantra to be used during meditation for 15 or 20 minutes twice a day. TM spokesmen say that the process allows the mind to experience a higher level of consciousness where thinking itself is transcended and the mind comes into direct contact with the primary source of all intelligence.

TM was instituted by the Indian guru, Maharishi Mahesh Yogi, in 1957, and it now has more than a million advocates throughout the world, hundreds of thousands in the U.S. alone. The technique is said to be an antidote to stress and the growing number of illnesses now found to be caused by same.

Scientific studies indicate that various physical changes do indeed occur during the act of meditation: an increase in alertness and electrical skin resistance; and a decrease in the rate of heartbeat, respiration, blood-pressure, and oxygen consumption. This state of being has been characterized as one of 'restful alertness' and sometimes as a fourth state of consciousness.

In his book, *TM – Discovering Inner Energy and Overcoming Stress*, Harold H. Bloomfield, M.D., describes an individual experiencing this condition: "His thinking mind quiets down into a wakeful state suffused with pure enjoyment. Cellular activity all over his body slows down, reducing his need for oxygen. Increasing relaxation permits increased flow of blood to his muscles, decreasing the heart's workload. Reduction in blood chemicals associated with tension and anxiety facilitates a sense of increased ease. Finally the cells of the brain fire in a synchronous manner, fostering integrated functioning between lower and higher brain centres and between left and right hemispheres."

Dr Bloomfield believes that TM, by integrating such brain functions, may foster the union of analytical and intuitive modes of thinking, thus resolving humanity's age-old struggle between emotion and reason.

Dr Bernard Glueck, a psychiatrist at the Institute of Living in Hartford, Ct., said: "It seems increasingly apparent from EEG findings that the mantra is the significant element in the whole process, apparently able to markedly alter brain function within a matter of seconds."

How does the mantra actually affect the brain – or the mind – or consciousness?

Om Mani Padme Hum

In his book, *The Only Dance There Is*, the author, Ram Dass, (otherwise known as Richard Alpert, Ph.D.), describes a mantra as a phrase that one repeats over and over again. He gives as an example the Tibetan phrase, *Om Mani Padme Hum*, as one of the most widely used mantras in the world today. "One of the ways of understanding its meaning," he writes, "is that *Om* means, like Brahma, that which is behind it all, the unmanifest. *Mani* means jewel or crystal. *Padme* means lotus and *Hum* means heart."

According to Ram Dass, one interpretation of the mantra might be, "God in unmanifest form is like a jewel in the middle of a lotus, manifest in my heart." After such a phrase is repeated for a long enough time to block out other thoughts, it apparently becomes a phenomenon unto itself.

"The conscious beings," writes Ram Dass, "who evolve certain languages such as Sanskrit specifically evolve the sounds of these languages to be connected with various states of consciousness – unlike the English language – so that a Sanskrit mantra, if you do it over and over again, will take you to a certain state of consciousness."

TM spokesmen, however, say that the technique will not work unless each student has his own mantra specifically chosen for him by a teacher personally trained by Maharishi.

Although transcendental meditation was regarded for some time essentially as an aid to relaxation, those who have taken it up seriously now see it as a boon, in fact *the* boon for humankind – with some unexpected psychic side effects and benefits.

Evolution of Consciousness

"The purpose of life is the evolution of consciousness," said one meditator, "and this takes place through the nervous system of which the brain is a part. The technique of transcendental meditation opens certain centres (or chakras) that speed up this evolutionary process, which leads eventually to that state known as enlightenment. And wonderful things may happen along the way: levitation, dematerialization, and even flying can occur. These phenomena, known as *siddhis*, are merely symptoms that one is advancing – they are signposts along the road to enlightenment."

At the time of this writing, there is a great deal of controversy about the 'flying and disappearing' abilities attributed to some meditators. The subject, for the most part, has been treated with a kind of humorous disbelief.

However, physicist Lawrence H. Domash, chancellor of Maharishi European Research University in Switzerland, states:

"As a scientist and particularly as a student of physics, I find it quite reasonable that the existing laws of nature have a level which comes into direct contact with human consciousness and which opens entirely new possibilities for the direct interaction of the mental and physical realms.

"Everything we know about scientific theory, especially in the past 50 years, points in this direction. After all, man has learned to fly already by a parallel procedure; to build a helicopter, one simply has to assemble some iron and glass and aluminium from under the ground in a specific way which depends upon knowledge of the appropriate natural laws. And then one can fly; nothing mysterious about it.

"The new and higher technology Maharishi is teaching today simply goes to a deeper level where consciousness and human physiology are involved directly rather than indirectly. I am confident that when the classic siddhis or supernormal powers are fully analysed, they will be seen to form a continuous extension of science rather than a contradiction to it."

Levitation of Saints and Mediums
Although this phenomenon is generally relegated to the world of Mary Poppins, Peter Pan, and Santa Claus's reindeer, history is filled with allusions to levitation, usually as occurrences in the lives of certain saints and spirit mediums. St Theresa of Avila was said to float in the air as she prayed, a situation that was remedied only when her skirts were held to the ground. And the famous 18th-century medium, Daniel Dunglas Home, stunned several continents with his levitations. Simon Magus (1st century A.D.) of biblical Samaria was reportedly able not only to levitate but to fly, until one day while demonstrating his powers, he plunged to his death from atop the Roman Forum.

The levitation of saints, incidentally, is presumed by theologians to be stationary, whereas the kind that involves transportation or actual flying is known as transvection and is usually attributed to witches.

Can human beings defy gravity and rise in the air? Those who say "yes" speak of a force within the individual that, like yeast, can cause the physical body to rise during states of higher consciousness. This force is not measurable, as a matter of fact it is perhaps best detected through its absence. After death, for example, without this power's leavening effect, the body becomes a "dead weight."

Others attribute what is called levitation to a certain yogic jump achieved by some after years of practice.

Source of Creative Intelligence
As mentioned earlier, TM spokesmen insist that such happenings are

mere sidelights and indications that one is on the true path towards enlightenment. In fact, TM itself is merely the technique of attaining what Maharishi calls the Source of Creative Intelligence. The meditation, say TM students, allows one to come in contact with the pure consciousness that is the basis of everything – the world of nature as well as the world of thought. When such contact is made regularly and frequently, there is a tendency toward order (a chaotic mental state becomes serene, for example).

I was told that with TM, smokers begin to smoke less and drinkers want fewer cocktails. And with this ordering of the mind, other advantages also occur. People seem to get *more* of whatever they need, be it sleep, success, or serenity when they begin tapping into this vat of pure consciousness.

Instrument to Save the World

Devotees of transcendental meditation believe it is the instrument that will save the world, citing the decrease in crime and improvement in human behaviour that they say occurs when a certain number of people meditate in each area. The following invitation, sent to all the governments of the world from the TM centre in Switzerland, illustrates the breadth and ambition of their aims:

"Scientific research of Transcendental Meditation conducted at more than two-hundred universities and research institutes in over 20 countries, including Germany, England, Canada, the U.S.A., Holland, India, South Africa, and Australia, during the last five years has repeatedly confirmed the personal experiences of hundreds and thousands of people all over the world that the physiology, psychology, and social behaviour of the individual become better with the regular practice of Transcendental Meditation.

"A preliminary study of 240 cities shows that when the number of people practising Transcendental Meditation reaches 1% of the city population, the crime rate drops dramatically, by an average of 17%. This statistical finding of the influence of Transcendental Meditation on both the individual and society has demonstrated the possibility for the creation of a better society than we are living in at present."[*]

Advocates say that transcendental meditation must be experienced in order to be fully understood.

---

[*] Dr Candace Borland, professor of education at Maharishi International University, is one of those who analyze statistics that relate TM to crime reduction.

Biofeedback

In biofeedback, machines are used to inform the user when he has mastered the control of his body's involuntary functions, such as heartbeat, blood-pressure, and allergic symptoms. In other words, it gives the subject's conscious mind the same kind of autonomy that hypnosis gives his unconscious. The machines, which include electroencephalographs, are wired to the subject's head while he is in meditation or practising various states of mind. His involuntary functions are then monitored and reported through light or sound signals. When the mental attitude or exercise produces the desired result, the machine signals. Therefore, biofeedback indicates the correct exercise or frame of mind for reducing blood pressure, allergy symptoms, or whatever the individual requires.

Mark Bricklin, in his previously quoted book, *The Practical Encyclopedia of Natural Healing,* describes how he witnessed a man well trained in biofeedback techniques jab a large sailmaker's needle into and through his upper arm. There was no pain and no blood.

Migraine Headache

Aside from the obvious benefits of conquering pain, biofeedback can be beneficial in more areas than one could possibly mention. Bricklin gives the "short-circuiting" of migraine headache attacks as one example. This is accomplished by people trained in biofeedback who can make their hands suddenly become warmer than usual; the blood that ordinarily engorges the vessels of the head in migraine is diverted to the hands and arms.

Why does biofeedback work? One theory is that it stimulates the right hemisphere of the brain (the non-verbal, feminine, subconscious hemisphere) into becoming more dominant – dominant enough for the left hemisphere (the verbal, male, conscious hemisphere) to become aware of its presence.

If this sounds like another feminist tract, consider Jack Leahy's comments in an article called 'Controlling the Mind,' which appeared in the June 1974 issue of *OP/The Osteopathic Physician.*

"According to medical specialists, perhaps as much as 80 per cent of human problems involve psychosomatic disease, either totally or as a contributing factor ... This means ... that a certain section of the brain ... the right hemisphere, learned a bad habit ... and is functioning in an undesirable manner. Research is showing that these bad habits can be voluntarily eliminated by retraining, using biofeedback to tell us what is happening in the physiological domain so that we can become aware of, and use, specific existential changes that are correlated with specific physiological changes.

"It seems reasonable to assume that if we can get physiologically sick from responding psychologically to stress in some inappropriate way, we can perhaps get well by learning to control the physiologic response. Feedback devices are important for this kind of learning because they mirror what is going on beneath the skin. Visual feedback tells us when our car is going off the road: biofeedback tells us about our bodies and allows us to make existential correction."

Biofeedback, then, through the use of machines, may achieve the marriage of the brain's right and left hemispheres in order to heal the body.

Breath Therapy

One of the easiest ways to feel the healing energy at work is to concentrate on each inhalation and exhalation of breath, noting its rhythm and quality, as well as any physical sensations that may accompany it.

One of the best breathing exercises I've come across is described in George Downing's *The Massage Book*. Downing suggests that breathing should be accompanied by a process known as 'centring.' This involves focusing your attention on the central part of your stomach and letting whatever you are doing – acting, feeling, seeing, talking – unfold itself from this central abdominal point.

According to Downing, you should imagine that your breath passes through and around this centre point and fills your entire body with each inhalation. This is best accomplished, he writes, by lying on your back in as relaxed a manner as possible. Then: "(1) Begin inhaling through the nose and exhaling out of the mouth. (2) Let your breath become as quiet, as smooth and as long as it wants to be without, however, forcing it in any manner. (3) After each exhalation, see if you can allow a pause to take place before inhaling again. Don't, however, do anything to actively 'hold' the breath out. Instead, just don't do anything at all to bring it back in – in other words, let yourself wait until the breath comes back entirely of its own accord. Don't worry about using the chest at all. Let each breath go straight to the abdomen. Explore how much space you can feel within your abdomen, and to what extent you can feel each inhalation filling that space.

A Step Further
"Next, if you would like to take this exercise a step further, add the following. (1) Continue with the same breathing pattern – in the nose and out the mouth, pausing after the exhalation, and letting each inhalation go all the way to the abdomen.

"(2) On every alternate breath, gently tighten your right buttock as you inhale. Make the movement as smooth as possible. Try to isolate the buttock muscles so that you are not flexing the muscles anywhere else in your body. At the same time, send your inhalation right into the buttock itself. (3) Release the buttock as you exhale, letting it settle into the floor as much as it wants ... Make this movement also as smooth as possible. At the same time, imagine that your exhalation is going right out the buttock itself.

"(4) Continue these two movements on every other breath. Rest, without moving, on the in-between breaths. (5) After several minutes move to your left buttock and repeat. (6) After doing the same on both sides, again let your breath simply filter down towards your abdomen, and see what sense of inner space you now can feel in this portion of your body.

"One last general clue: don't fall into the trap of trying to separate 'physical sensations' from 'emotional qualities.' To tune in to the energy which is your body is to feel neither just the one nor just the other, but the common root of both."

Psychiatrists of the neo-Reichian school are strong advocates of breath therapy. One of the first things they alert patients suffering from depression to, for example, is the quality of their breathing, which is nearly always shallow. Deep breathing in fresh air was of paramount importance to Reich himself, and is one of the fastest, easiest, and least expensive ways to put oneself in touch with the energy that heals.

Exercise Therapy

It is very difficult to separate exercise therapy from breath therapy, since the two are so intertwined. The distinction is really a matter of emphasis.

One of the reasons that certain forms of sport, especially skiing, have become so addictive is that the body is literally flooded with energy (orgone, or *ch'i*, or whatever one wishes to call it) through the type of breathing and exercise involved. Among the things that made the film *Rocky* so popular were the jogging scenes. Audiences, through a kind of osmosis, seemed to feel the energy flow portrayed on the screen, and some reported a strong sense of physical well-being after leaving theatre.

Jogging, incidentally, if employed judiciously, produces an accelerated flow of this energy that science cannot 'see,' yet everyone can feel. Our bodies are veritable fields of energy, always in a state of change, always moving towards aliveness or deadness.

One exercise instructress I talked with is convinced that the healing energy plays a much greater part in our lives than anyone could guess.

"It is not the exercise alone that makes my clients feel better and look better. It is the fact that curious energy that seemed lost with their youth comes rising to the surface again. Their mental attitudes change from negative to positive. Many have found that they no longer need their psychiatrists. No, it's not the exercise alone that does it; it's the energy that heals."

But it is my feeling that the exercise somehow triggers this vital force, just as music can. Dancers, who are involved with both music and exercise during so much of their lives, are very aware of this energy's flow. But there are many who can tune into it, so to speak, through music alone.

Music Therapy

Most people are aware of the tingling sensation that can be aroused by good music, but few are aware of its healing nature. Yet music as medicine is as old as Apollo, who was the Greek god of both. Francis Bacon wrote: "The poets did well to conjoin music and medicine in Apollo, because the office of medicine is but to tune this curious harp of man's body and to reduce it to harmony."

In an earlier chapter, it was cited that the healing rituals of the Pythagoreans involved music as a means of restoring health when mental or physical harmony was disturbed. And Mesmer, discussed in Chapter 5, believed music to be a potent medium for the conveyance of the energy called animal magnetism. This is why he conducted his treatment to the accompaniment of music played on the piano or glass harmonica, an instrument made of rotating glass cylinders that produced tones when rubbed by wet fingers. A change of key or meter could cause spasms in his patients who, during treatment, were highly sensitive to music.

A publication called *Medicine and Music,* from the National Library of Medicine, Bethesda, Md., reports that the 6th-century philosopher, Boethius, divided music into three types: "musica mundana," or the relations of the cosmic bodies; "musica humana," the workings of the human body and soul; and "musica instrumentalis," or composed music, both instrumental and vocal.

Four Modes of Music

The 16th-century composer, Gioseffo Zarlineo, decided that just as the world was created of four elements and the body of four humours, so music was made up of four modes; each of these was related to one of the elements and to one of the humours: one to fire and yellow bile; another to water and phlegm; a third to air and blood; and still another to earth and black bile.

The humoral theory of health, prevalent until the latter part of the 18th century, believed that the predominance of any one bodily humour, or fluid, affected both mind and body. A surplus of black bile produced a melancholic temperament, as well as genius; yellow bile was responsible for the choleric or irritable individual; phlegm caused listlessness; and when blood dominates, the temperament is sanguine. Corresponding physical complaints are biliousness associated with both black and yellow bile, haemorrhage with blood, and colds with phlegm.

Since health depended upon a balanced correspondence among the four humours, Zarlineo felt such harmony could be restored by music in the proper mode.

Effect of Music on the Humours

Athanasius Kircher, a 17th-century German doctor and scientist, further advanced Zarlineo's theory. And he demonstrated the effect of music on the humours by means of glasses, each filled with a different liquid having what he presumed to be the character of one of the humours. When the rims of the glasses were rubbed by moistened fingers, producing musical tones, each fluid was set in a different degree of motion. And each humour was moved by one special tone.

Music, Kircher concluded, moved the bodily fluids or humours by means of reverberations of the outer air, which, in turn, moved the inner air or "animal spirits" present in the ear. These spirits carried the reverberations in the blood stream throughout the body. The consonance and dissonance, tempo, pitch, melodic intervals, and dynamics of the music had their special effects upon the movements of the animal spirits; and each variation of movement produced a different mood.

According to *Medicine and Music*, the muscles and nerves were moved by the animal spirits, but they were also affected directly by the music. The nervous system, said Kircher, was stretched like a series of strings along a wooden sound board, and the "fibres" vibrated in sympathy when a tone "proportional" to them was sounded.

Later experimentation found that pulse, blood-pressure, and breathing were all demonstrably affected by the various components of which music is made: rhythm, dissonance and consonance, pitch and loudness.

Music in Mental Hospitals

Today, music is, alas, one of the unsung heroines of modern therapeutics. Aside from its use in mental hospitals, it is rarely employed. Interestingly enough, within the field of mental illness it has been found that even the most profoundly disturbed patients, those who seem completely oblivious to their surroundings respond to the rhythmical element of melody. (They also respond to the moon and all of its various phases. Since the moon controls the tides of our oceans, some believe that it also exerts a pull on the fluids within our bodies. This, too, like music, is a matter of rhythm, and one is reminded of the harmony of the spheres described by Pythagoras, Paracelsus, and others.)

There can be little doubt that music soothes. It also, somehow, evokes the healing energy. This may occur through its ability to create meditative states that relax the brain's left hemisphere and stimulate its right.

The therapies discussed fall into three categories: (1) Those that concentrate on the use of the *ch'i* energy and the rebalancing of *yin* and *yang* principles (acupuncture, *t'ai-chi, shiatsu, jin shin jyutsu,* and reflexology).

(2) Those that seem to employ the energy known as orgone (Reichian therapeutics, bioenergetics, breath therapy, and simple exercise).

(3) Those that produce meditative states and may use prana, as well as somehow affecting the hemispheres of the brain.

Ch'i, prana, orgone ... the mystery remains.

12

TOWARDS A NEW ERA OF HEALING

Medicine of the future will be preventive and holistic. It will build health as well as treat disease. And it will consider the human being not as a machine with interchangeable parts but as a trilogy of body, mind, and spirit.

Certainly, traditional medicine has not neglected preventive medicine; the vaccines now available against formerly fatal diseases have prolonged human life to an inestimable degree. And further study in pathology and the dynamics of disease continues to be of the utmost importance.

As a supplement to traditional healing, the holistic approach will persevere in its focus on maintaining harmony among the physical organs and their functions in order to ward off illness. Where disease already exists, holistic medicine will strive to restore the individual's health to a point where he is able to use his own healing energy to reject the threatening influence, bacteria or other.

Traditional medicine adheres, by and large, to the germ theory of disease. The holistic healer, although he recognizes that bacterial or viral infection is present during illness, is apt to postulate that germs alone do not *cause* disease but move in only when the individual is in a poor state of health with weakened powers of resistance. It is the holistic doctor's goal to maintain his patients in a stable condition of physical well-being.

Negative States of Mind

What constitutes good health? Most people are aware of the need for proper nutrition, sleep, and exercise in order to keep themselves fit. But the effects of mental-emotional states on the body are less well known. The fact is that diseases such as arthritis, allergies, strokes, diabetes, heart ailments, glandular malfunctions, ulcers, and even cancer have all been linked to negative states of mind. Future healers will lay greater emphasis on the authority of mind over body and its ability to kill or cure.

The body itself now appears to be a system of energy as much as – and perhaps even more than – a system of tissue, bone, and cell (mass). And holistic doctors treat the body *as* energy as well as mass. There can, therefore, be little doubt that this energy – call it orgone, *ch'i, mana*, prana, Innate, or vital force – does indeed exist. It is, after all, presently being harnessed, or released from blockage, by the various therapies of acupuncture, homoeopathy, bioenergetics, kinesiology, hypnosis, chiropractic, yoga, psychic healing, biofeedback and others.

The healing energy can be harnessed, yes, but still not scientifically measured. In essence it continues to be a mystery, perhaps because it is so inextricably linked with the human soul, a phenomenon largely rejected by rational science seven centuries ago. It cannot be denied that this rationalism led to concise medical observation, which engendered great advances in the fields of surgery and drugs. It also led to specialization and a view of man as a system of parts. Future medicine will enlarge that view into a perception of the human being as a whole, a unified complex of body, mind, and soul.

Continuous Life-Spans

Oriental doctors are accustomed to the spiritual component in healing, primarily because most of them have accepted reincarnation as a fact. The concept of soul as a traveller of continuous life-spans allows an easy receptivity to the idea of a spiritual reality in all areas, not excluding that of medicine. Furthermore, the practice of acupuncture and its success have allowed them to recognize the reality of *ch'i* without having to see it under a microscope.

A most promising sign is the fact that acupuncture now flourishes on Western shores. Its continued success may compel even the most sceptical intellects to acknowledge the healing energy, at least the variety known as *ch'i*.

Holistic doctors, when they discuss the spiritual aspect of the body-mind-spirit triad, often sound more Eastern than Western in their approach. Dr Paavo Airola, in the June 1977 issue of *Let's Live* magazine, writes: "Our life on this planet, at this time in history, is just a short episode in the eternal divine plan of human development and progression – a schooling period aimed at improving and perfecting our human and divine characteristics.

Divine Nature and Purpose

"Although in my articles, books, and lectures, I deal mostly with nutritional and other physical aspects of preventing disease and restoring health, I wish to emphasize that there is a divine nature and purpose to all life, and that the real reason for achieving good health and building a strong, healthy body is to prepare a way for our spiritual growth and perfection.

"Freed from disease and pain, we can pursue our true purpose in life – the perfection and refinement of our divine spirit. Only when our efforts to improve physical health are thus motivated will they fit into the framework of the purposeful, divinely designed plan for our lives."

When one believes that the body is the dwelling place of an evolving soul, life seems to make more sense, and one's mental attitude becomes brighter. And when one's mental attitude is brighter, one's physical health improves: body, mind, spirit.

Consider the disease of depression, which may afflict as many as 15 million people in the United States alone. Although symptoms may vary in his body, the true state of the depressive's mind was well described by Macbeth when he observed life to be no more than a tale told by an idiot, full of sound and fury, signifying nothing; and better still by Hamlet when he sighed: "How weary, stale, flat, and unprofitable seem to me all the uses of this world."

Such an attitude is rarely sustained by those who believe in reincarnation. And although most holistic doctors would be loath to impose new religious beliefs upon their patients, there are times when a strong conviction of the soul's immortality may be the only deterrent to suicide. It is only when a person stops wanting to die, after all, that he begins to take care of his body.

Other holistic approaches to depression might be through the rebalancing of a patient's biochemistry with a corrected diet and megavitamin therapy: or through the daily practice of the neo-Reichian bioenergetics; or through homoeopathic remedies. There are a number of paths toward the reharmony of body, mind, spirit.

Steiner and Anthroposophy

One of the most profound and articulate advocates of the premise that health is spiritual was the Austrian philosopher, Rudolf Steiner, 1861-1925. Steiner, who founded the spiritual science known as anthroposophy, received the respect of a large section of the medical community; and a favourable article about him appeared as recently as February 1969, in the American magazine, *MD*. Called 'Scientific Seer,' the article described him thus:

"A strange and controversial figure during the early decades of this century was the Austrian philosopher-occultist Rudolf Steiner, whose name became a household word in German-speaking countries.

"An editor of Goethe's works, friend of the biologist Ernst Haeckel, Steiner taught that psychic powers could be used with scientific precision to restore humanism to a materialistic world. He warned that if they were not so used, either human feeling would succumb to the ever increasing demands of mechanical efficiency or people would try to escape from these demands into neurotic private worlds.

"Gifted with what he claimed to be spiritual perception, Steiner declared that this was nothing out of the ordinary, that an enhanced consciousness was latent in every man and could be awakened through proper training. Out of this belief he formulated a distinctive 'spiritual science' which he called anthroposophy, the higher wisdom of humanity, by which he explained the nature of the world in terms of human nature."

Steiner believed that the soul could be used scientifically to revive humanism in a mechanistic and materialistic world. And he was convinced that the gap between the spiritual and the scientific could be bridged.

Organs of Spiritual Sight

In *An Outline of Anthroposophical Medical Research*, Steiner said that the spiritual part of man, to the trained observer, was as visible as the physical. But these organs of spiritual sight, he added, could be brought about only if one unfolded within himself an earnest life of thought.

"Such a state of living, of resting in quietude – in thought – must, however, be carried out so as to bring about a methodical education and transformation of the soul. If one can, so to say, experiment for a time with one's own soul, allowing it to rest within an easily grasped thought, at the same time permitting neither any traces of auto-suggestion nor any diminution of consciousness to arise, and if one in this way exercises the soul as one would exercise a muscle, then the soul grows strong. Methodically, one pursues the exercises further and further; the soul grows stronger, grows powerful, and becomes *capable of sight.*

"The first thing that it sees is that the human being actually does not consist merely of a physical body, which can be investigated either with the naked eye or with a microscope, and so forth, but that he also bears an etheric body ... It is something that can really be perceived and observed; and if I were to distinguish qualitatively between the physical body and the etheric body, I should choose, out of all the innumerable qualitative distinctions that exist, the following: the physical body of man is subject to the laws of gravity; it tends to be drawn earthward. The etheric body tends to be drawn towards the periphery of the universe; that is to say, outwards, in all directions. As a rule, our investigations are concerned with the relative weight of things, but that part of the human organism which possesses weight is the direct opposite of that which not only has no weight but which strives to escape from the laws of gravitation. We have in us these two opposing forces."

The Astral Body
Steiner believed that man consisted of a third body as well, which he called the astral. It is through the astral body, he said, that man possesses consciousness and is able to experience emotion and desire. The astral body interpenetrates both the etheric and physical bodies of man; it is also found in the animal world functioning at a more impersonal and less specific level.

The three bodies, Steiner taught, must relate harmoniously with one another and with the ego in order for health to be maintained. His definition of the ego or ego-organization, however, is not to be confused with Freud's. To Steiner it was "the whole of those attributes of the human being by means of which he attains his sense of '*I am.*' As hearing, sight, taste, etc., each have their 'organs' of expression, so also has the ego. In this case the 'organ' is the entire physical body in its self-conscious contact with the outer world."

According to Steiner, only man contains the four phenomena of ego plus astral, etheric, and physical bodies; animals possess the astral, etheric, and physical; plants have the etheric and physical; and minerals are involved with the physical only.

Anabolic and Katabolic Forces

For several years, Steiner lectured on anatomy, physiology, pathology, and therapeutics to a class of over forty doctors and medical students. According to *A Scientist of the Invisible* by A.P. Shepherd, "The first point that Steiner established in the physiology of the human being was that man manifests continually, all through his life, the presence of two forces within his body that are polarically opposed and that need to be held in balance by a continuous process of adjustment. These are the anabolic and katabolic forces, the forces of growth and decay, the forces by which the body is built up and those by which it is destroyed, the forces of physical life and death."

Steiner believed that these counteracting forces functioned through the interplay of the four members of man's being described above: the physical body, the etheric body, the astral body, and the ego. Health, he said, depends upon the general balance throughout the body between these forces of health and decay. Illness is the disturbance of this harmony, a disturbance that arises essentially out of the distortion of balance in the human soul and spirit.

Shepherd writes: "The powers of Thinking (Ego), having lost the sense of their pure relation to the spirit, have associated themselves in purely Intellectual Thinking (Ego-Astral) with the instincts of Life and Growth (the Etheric) in the lower bodily nature of man – as centred on and satisfied by the material world – and the feeling-life arising out of that lower nature. Thus the origin of the physical unbalance called disease would be related to the human spiritual unbalance, scientific materialism."

Remedies that Restore Balance

Anthroposophical medicine includes remedies that restore balance, either by curbing the overactive forces or by stimulating those that are lacking. The lack of balance between the astral and etheric forces, writes Shepherd, is best dealt with by plant remedies; that between the ego and the astral, by mineral remedies.

Steiner did *not* believe that all illness was an outside evil that could be removed by spiritual forces. He said that illness arises in a lack of balance, in an endless fluctuation between integration and disintegration, without which there could be neither life nor spirit-consciousness.

There are many highly qualified physicians in the United States,

Germany, Switzerland, and elsewhere who are practising anthroposophical medicine. Elaborating on Steiner's healing methods, Dr Ita Wegman writes in the Swiss publication, *Natura*:*

"Health means that the four members of man (physical body, etheric body, astral body and ego-organization) work together in harmony. Each organ must have the right connection with its etheric and astral forces. If this is not the case, then illness arises. And it is actually always the astral body which causes the disease ...

"If the activities of the astral body are too one-sided and disordered, then they can cause destructive processes in the particular organ. This happens at that moment when there is disharmony between the etheric and astral forces, when the astral is too closely connected with the physical and life processes, i.e., where the etheric could not fully develop.

"This sort of disharmony can have two causes. Either the etheric body is naturally weak which is usually connected with hereditary factors and a delicate constitution and can lead to chronic illnesses, or the astral body is too active and independent because the spiritual ego-organization is not closely enough connected with it."

Spiritual Origins

Steiner's medical philosophy was rooted in the tenet that human beings have spiritual origins. Each individual was the vehicle for an evolving spirit that reached far beyond the boundaries of life and death. And he was perhaps one of the few reincarnationists who were totally committed to the basic tenets of Christianity.

Steiner immersed himself in a study of Christianity that was spiritual as well as historic, and evolved a line of thinking that became the mainspring of his life; to him the Incarnation became the pivotal fact in all history, human and divine, while the death of Christ was a mystic fact that interpreted all history before it and affected every aspect of earthly life after it ... he developed the concept that Christ's life on earth was the central focal point towards which all the past had been leading and from which all the future was to take form and evolve along the path to freedom, self-awareness and love. To him the ancient mysteries were steps along the way to the ultimate revelation, the earthlife of Christ.

---

* Reprinted in *The Art of Healing*, edited by A.E. Abbott.

Steiner was convinced that a spiritual science was necessary in order to prevent the mental decay and corruption that take root in an overly mechanized world. And his philosophy was (and is) uniquely attuned to Western society.

Oriental Religions

It is ironic, therefore, and totally antithetical to his tenets* that today, in an attempt to escape the mechanization and demoralization described by Steiner, hordes of young people raised in the tradition of Western culture, are now turning to Eastern spiritual disciplines for meaning. The Oriental religions, they say, not only allow them to transcend a society which they find, for the most part, materialistic and depraved, but also replace it with something of value.

Instead of listening to repetitious sermons from a man in a pulpit, they are, these young people say, actively involved in day-to-day rituals of meditation and exercise that fulfil them in body, mind, and soul. It is not surprising that holistic medicine thrives in the communities that house such seekers. At the yoga centres known as ashrams, for example, one frequently finds holistic health clinics that include yoga in their therapeutics.

The healing energy released through yoga is known as prana. And the technique of controlling it is called pranayama, which is a system of breathing techniques. Pranayama is considered a highly sophisticated practice, which must be supervised by a teacher. After long training, the student may acquire the ability to guide the healing pranic energy to specific internal organs. And with prolonged practice, he may be able to channel the prana in order to achieve what some call cosmic consciousness.

Russian Parapsychological Research

Although holistic medicine, as practiced in ashrams and elsewhere in the United States, will utilize the concepts of both soul and healing energy, it may be the Russians who will first establish their scientific reality. They spend millions of dollars annually on parapsychological

---

* Steiner wished to separate occult studies from their Oriental affiliations. He believed that the only occultism of value to the Western world must differ greatly from that taught in ancient mystery schools before the dawn of Christianity. Although he held the greatest respect for such ancient wisdom, Steiner felt that the modern Western world, with its emphasis on individual responsibility, would be best served by a scientific approach to spirituality (or anthroposophy).

research, and Soviet scientists apparently take the subject far more seriously than do ours. It is to be fervently hoped, however, that they discover the existence of the human soul *before* they harness the energy. For the energy that heals, as we have learned from earlier chapters, could be transformed into the energy that destroys.

An article called 'Emigré Tells of Research in Soviet in Parapsychology for Military Use,' by Flora Lewis, appeared in *The New York Times* on June 19, 1977. After describing a report that the Soviet Union has been doing secret work in parapsychology for what appears to be military purposes, the article states that on June 13, 1975, the Soviet leader, Leonid Brezhnev, "urged the United States to agree on a ban on research and development of new kinds of weapons 'more terrible' than anything the world has known. American arms control negotiators have tried to find out from their Soviet counterparts what he had in mind, but they have not learned anything more than that he meant 'some kind of rays,' according to United States officials."

Articles such as these cannot help but reinforce one's conviction that the world is in need of some universal morality that would preclude the proliferation of death weapons. Science without religion has offered no solace but the balance of terror.

Reincarnation

It is unfortunate that Western religion presents no guarantees for the benign use of the healing energy. The retribution, immortality, and eternal life stressed in the Bible seem rather ambiguous to a growing majority. According to some sources, the more concice policy of reincarnation was an actual part of the early Christian church until the Council of Constantinople in 553 A.D. abandoned the idea as being too complex for the masses. In any event, there is nothing in the Bible that says reincarnation is untrue.

Reincarnation is a view, incidentally, that has been held by such scientific minds as Thomas Edison, Benjamin Franklin, and even that great logician, Immanuel Kant. Any system of metaphysical belief that improves the quality of life must be for the good. And even the most sceptical minds might heed the advice of the German philosopher, Hans Vaihinger, who said that in such cases it is wiser to behave "as if" something exists even when one cannot *know* that it actually does.

Progressive Revelation

Let us suppose that it is the year 2001, and we have survived. The reason for this is that war, finally, has been banned. This resolution was brought about by a sudden, almost universal acceptance of the Baha'i faith, which acknowledges all religions and their various systems of afterlife. The Baha'is believe in progressive revelation. Abraham, Christ, Moses, Mohammed, Zoroaster, Buddha, and others, they say, were all part of the divine plan. The revelation of their own prophet, Baha'u'llah, is simply the most recent of the divinely revealed religions, and fulfills the ancient promise of spiritual unity with dictates that are crucial to the problems of this era.

Bah'u'llah's religious principles include adoption of an international auxiliary language; a world economy; a world legislature; a world tribunal; equality of men and women; universal compulsory education; independent investigation of truth; agreement between science and religion; universal faith based on the foundations of great religions; and a world union governed by the representatives of all people.

With the balance of terror replaced by a positive and benign philosophy that recognizes all religions, as well as the reality and migrating nature of the human soul, spiritual and mental health have been universally improved. Despair, both existential and specific, has been dislodged by hope.

In the holistic health centres, x-rays have been replaced by Kirlian photography, which diagnoses disease through its photograph of the aura, a now proven phenomenon. Other diagnostic techniques, including reflexology, allow illness to be observed before it becomes serious, and therapeutic measures treat the energy body more often than the physical one. Nutrition is of prime importance. The biochemical nature of many mental illnesses has been recognized, and megavitamin therapy is now widespread. In fact, individual biochemistry is determined at birth, and each person's dietary needs are diagnosed accordingly.

Because we are now altogether a more co-operative than competitive people, optimum health care – physical, mental, and spiritual – is available to all. Some attribute this to food processing for health rather than profits; others credit the new clean-air projects and the lessening of general stress.

Holistic health standards are inherent in the growing number of schools based on the educational concepts of Pythagoras and Rudolf

Steiner* — concepts that remove anxiety from the faces of children. Tension-reducers such as alcohol, cigarettes, and tranquillizers have been replaced by meditation, as well as exercise and breathing techniques.

Individuals now see themselves as developing spirits within a collective, universal evolution of consciousness. There is a great joy and excitement within this recognition. And the 'highs' resulting from the techniques that aid one's climb towards awareness are found to be more powerful than those formerly achieved through drugs.

All of the therapies described in the previous chapter have become commonplace, as has all holistic medicine. And through some gracious alchemy, the harmony of body-mind-soul within each man has led to a growing harmony between all men. In this future state, philosophy, science, and religion are aligned once again. And the healing energy abounds both within and without.

If this sounds utopian, let us consider the alternative. It is 2001, and we have continued on as we are today. Our leaders have, inevitably, quarrelled, and bombs have, inevitably, been dropped. The survivors are not much concerned with medicine, holistic or other. The world is a dark place, and the only energy in evidence is not that which heals.

* At the time of this writing, there are 165 Rudolf Steiner schools (called Waldorf schools) throughout the world. Here, children are educated to feel as well as think, and mind is not split from body.

BIBLIOGRAPHY

Aaronson, Bernard, and Osmond, Humphrey; *Psychedelics* (Garden City, New York: Doubleday, 1970).

Abbot, A.E. (editor); *The Art of Healing* (London: Emerson Press, 1963).

Airola, Paavo; 'The Total Approach to Health and Healing,' *Let's Live* (Los Angeles, Ca.: Oxford Industries, June 1977).

Bach, Marcus; *The Chiropractic Story* (Austell, Georgia: Si-Nel Publishing, 1968).

Bean, Orson; *Me and the Orgone* (New York: Macmillan, 1971).

Beau, Georges; *Chinese Medicine* (New York: Hearst; Avon Division, 1975).

Becker, Ernest; *The Denial of Death* (New York: Macmillan, 1975).

Bentov, Itzhak; *Stalking the Wild Pendulum* (New York: Dutton, 1977).

Bidwell, G.I.; *How to Use the Repertory* (London: Homoeopathic Publishing Co.).

Bleibture, John N.; *The Parable of the Beast* (New York: Collier, 1971).

Bloomfield, R. Harold; Cain, Michael; Jaffe, Dennis; *TM* (New York: Delacorte Press, 1975).

Bragdon, Claude; *Yoga for You* (New York: Lancer).

Brena, Steven F.; *Yoga & Medicine* (New York: Penguin, 1976).

Bricklin, Mark; *Natural Healing* (Emmaus, Pa.: Rodale Press, 1976).

Campbell, Anthony; *Seven States of Consciousness* (New York: Harper and Row, 1974).

Capra, Fritjof; *The Tao of Physics* (Berkeley, Ca.: Shabhala, 1975).

Carter, Mary Ellen, and McGarey, William; *Edgar Cayce on Healing* (New York: Coronet, 1972).

Chambers, John D. (translator); *The Divine Pymander and Other Writings of Hermes Trismegistus* (New York: Samuel Weiser, 1972).

Close, Stuart: *The Genius of Homoeopathy* (Calcutta: Haren & Brother, 1967).

Connelly, Dianne M.; *Traditional Acupuncture: The Law of the Five Elements* (Columbia, Maryland: Centre for Traditional Acupuncture, Inc., 1975).

Denniston, Denise, and McWilliams, Peter: *The TM Book* (Allen Park, Mich.: Three Rivers Press, 1975).

De Ropp, Robert S.; *The Master Game* (New York: Dell, 1968).

Downing, George; *The Massage Book* (New York: Random House, 1972).

Esslemont, J.E.; *Baha'u'llah and the New Era* (Wilmette, Ill.: Baha'i Books, 1970).

Faraday, Dr Ann; *Dream Power* (New York: Coward, McCann, 1972).

Gallert, Dr Mark; *New Light on Therapeutic Energies* (London: James Clarke & Co., 1966).

Gamow, George; *Thirty Years That Shook Physics* (Garden City, New York: Doubleday; Anchor Books Division, 1966).

Germain, Walter; *The Magic Power of Your Mind* (New York: Hawthorn Books, 1956).

Govinda, Lama Anagarika; *Foundations of Tibetan Mysticism* (New York: Samuel Weiser, 1972).

Graves, Robert; *The White Goddess* (New York: Farrar, Straus and Giroux, 1970).

Greenfield, Jerome; *Wilhelm Reich vs. the U.S.A.* (New York: Norton, 1974).

Gutman, William; *Modern Medicine and Homoeopathy* (New York: Foundation for Homoeopathic Research. Inc.).

Hahnemann, Dr Samuel; *Organon of Medicine* (Calcutta: M. Bhattacharyya & Co.).

Hall, Manly P.; *The Mystical and Medical Philosophy of Paracelsus* (Los Angeles: Philosophical Research Society, 1964).

Heisenberg, Werner; *Physics and Philosophy* (New York: Harper & Row, 1958).

Hewitt, James; *Yoga and You* (New York: Pyramid Books, 1967).

Hisey, Lehmann; *Keys to Inner Space* (New York: Avon Books, 1974).

Hoffman, Enid; *Huna* (Gloucester, Mass.: Para Research, 1976).

Ilich, Ivan; *Medical Nemesis* (New York: Random House; Pantheon Division, 1976).

Isaacs, James, and Lamb, John; *Complementarity in Biology* (Baltimore: Johns Hopkins Press, 1969).

James, William; *The Varieties of Religious Experience* (New York: Macmillan, 1961).

Jaynes, Julian; *The Origin of Consciousness in the Breakdown of the Bicameral Mind* (Boston: Houghton Mifflin, 1977).

Jensen, Bernard; *World Keys to Health & Long Life* (Escondido, Ca.: Omni Publishers, 1975).

Jung, Carl; *Man and His Symbols* (New York: Doubleday, 1969).

Jurgen, Thorwald; *Science and Secrets of Early Medicine* (New York: Harcourt, Brace and World, 1963).

Kent, James Tyler; *Lectures on Homoeopathic Materia Medica* (Philadelphia: Boericke & Tafel, 1911).

Koestler, Arthur; *The Roots of Coincidence* (New York: Random House, 1973).

Kroeger, Rev. Hanna; *The Pendulum, the Bible, and Your Survival* (Boulder, Col.: 1973).

Kruger, Helen; *Other Healers, Other Cures* (Indianapolis/New York: Bobbs-Merrill, 1974).

Kuhn, Thomas; *The Structure of Scientific Revolutions* (Chicago & London: University of Chicago Press, 1969).

Kurtz, Ron, and Prestera, Dr Hector; *The Body Reveals* (New York: Harper & Row, 1976).

Law, Donald; *A Guide to Alternative Medicine* (London: Turnstone Press, 1974).

LeShan, Lawrence; *How to Meditate* (New York: Bantam, 1975).

Libby, Walter; *The History of Medicine* (Boston: Houghton Mifflin).

Ligeros, Kleanthes; *How Ancient Healing Governs Modern Therapeutics* (New York: G.P. Putnam's Sons).

Long, Max Freedom; *The Secret Science Behind Miracles* (Marina del Rey, Ca.: DeVorss & Company).

Lowen, Alexander; *Bioenergetics* (New York: Penguin Books, 1975).

Lucas, Richard; *Nature's Medicines* (New York: Award Books, 1966).

Maharishi European Research University; *Enlightenment and the*

Siddhis (Lake Lucerne, Switzerland: MERU Press, 1977).

Maharishi International University; *Inauguration of the Dawn of the Age of Enlightenment* (West Germany: MIU Press, 1975).

Mann, W. Edward; *Orgone, Reich & Eros* (New York: Simon and Schuster; Touchstone Books, 1973).

Marti-Ibanez, Felix; *Centaur Essays on the History of Medical Ideas* (New York: MD Publications).

Martin, P.W.; *Experiment in Depth* (London: Routledge & Kegan Paul, 1964).

Medicine and Music, (National Library of Medicine, DHEW Publication No. (NIH) 77-1411).

Meek, George W.; *From Enigma to Science* (New York: Samuel Weiser, 1973).

Moody, Dr Raymond A., Jr.; *Life After Life* (New York: Bantam, 1976).

Myers, F.W.H.; *Human Personality and Its Survival of Bodily Death*, edited by Susy Smith (New Hyde Park, N.Y.: University Books, 1961).

Nash, E.B.; *Leaders in Homoeopathic Therapeutics* (Calcutta; M. Bhattacharyya & Co., 1971).

Nielsen, Greg, and Polansky, Joseph; *Pendulum Power* (New York: Destiny Books, 1977).

Ostrander, Sheila, and Schroeder, Lynn; *Psychic Discoveries Behind the Iron Curtain* (New York: Prentice-Hall, 1970).

Ostrander, Sheila, and Schroeder, Lynn; *Handbook of Psi Discoveries* (New York: Berkeley Publishing Corp., 1974).

Oyle, Dr Irving; *The Healing Mind* (Millbrae, Ca.: Celestial Arts, 1975).

Palermo, Richard A.; *Chiropractic, A View from Within* (St James, N.Y.: Dr Richard A. Palermo, 1976).

Palos, Stephan; *The Chinese Art of Healing* (New York: Bantam, 1972).

Paracelsus; *Paracelsus, Selected Writings*, edited by Jolande Jacobi, translated by Norbert Guterman (Princeton, N.J.: Princeton University Press; Bollingen Foundation, 1973).

Pauling, Linus; 'Orthomolecular Psychiatry,' *Science* (New York: Vol 190, April 19, 1968).

Pawlak, Vic; *Megavitamin Therapy and the Drug Wipeout Syndrome* (Phoenix, Arizona: Do It Now Foundation, 1972).

Pelletier, Kenneth R.; *Mind as Healer, Mind as Slayer* (New York: Dell; Delta Division, 1977).

Plato; *Great Dialogues of Plato*, translated by W.H.D. Rouse; edited by Eric H. Warmington and Philip G. Rouse (New York: Mentor).

Podmore, Frank; *From Mesmer to Christian Science* (New Hyde Park, N.Y.: University Books, 1964).

Ram Dass; *The Only Dance There Is* (Garden City, NY.: Anchor Press/Doubleday, 1974).

Rapport, Samuel; *Great Adventures in Medicine* (New York: Dial Press).

Read, Anne; Ilstrup, Carol; Gammon, Margaret; *Edgar Cayce on Diet and Health* (New York: Warner, 1973).

Regush, Nicholas M., editor; *Frontiers of Healing* (New York: Avon, 1977).

Reich, Ilse Ollendorff; *Wilhelm Reich; a Personal Biography* (New York: St Martin's Press, 1969).

Reich, Wilhelm; *Selected Writings, An Introduction to Orgonomy* (New York: Farrar, Straus and Giroux, 1960).

Robertson, J.M.; *Pagan Christs* (New Hyde Park, N.Y.: University Books, 1967).

Santesson, Hans Stefen; *Reincarnation* (New York: Award Books, 1969).

'Scientific Seer: Rudolf Steiner,' *MD* (MD Publications, February 1969).

Segal, Maybelle; *Reflexology* (Ardmore, Pa.: Whitmore Publishing, 1976).

Shepherd, A.P., *A Scientist of the Invisible*   (New York: Inner Traditions International, Ltd., 1983)

Sigenist, Henry E.; *A History of Medicine* (New York: Oxford University Press, 1961).

Singer, June; Androgyny (Garden City, N.Y.: Anchor Press/Doubleday, 1976).

Smith, Homer W.; *Man and His Gods* (New York: Grosset & Dunlap, 1957).

Smith, Huston; *The Religions of Man* (New York: Mentor, 1958).

Snodgrass, Kelley; 'Chiropractic,' *East West Journal* (Boston: August, 1976).

Steiner Rudolf; *An Outline of Anthroposophical Medical Research* (London: Rudolf Steiner Publishing Co.).

Steiner Rudolf; *Fundamentals of Therapy* (London: Anthroposophical Publishing Co.).

Stelter, Alfred; *Psi Healing*, translated by Ruth Hein (New York: Bantam, 1976).

Southard, C.O.; *Truth Ideas of an M.D.* (Lee's Summit, Mo.: Unity, 1958).

Sugrue, Thomas; *There is a River* (New York: Dell, 1966).

Teeguarden, Ron and Iona, 'Jin Shin Jyutsu,' *East West Journal* (Boston: October, 1974).

Thie, John F., with Marks, Mary; *Touch for Health* (Santa Monica, Ca.: DeVorss & Co., 1973).

Tilden, John H.; *Toxemia, the Basic Cause of Disease* (Chicago: Natural Hygiene Press, 1974).

Valentine, Tom; *Psychic Surgery* (New York: Pocket Books, 1975).

Von Reichenbach, Baron Karl; *The Mysterious Odic Force* (The Aquarian Press, 1977).

Von Reichenbach, Baron Karl; *Researches on Magnetism, Electricity, Heat, Light, Crystallization and Chemical Attraction in Relation to the Vital Force* (Secaucus, N.J.: University Books, 1974).

Walker, Kenneth M.; *The Story of Medicine* (New York: Oxford University Press, 1955).

Westlake, Aubrey T., M.D.; *The Pattern of Health* (Berkeley, Ca.: Shambhala Publications, 1974).

Wilson, Colin; *The Occult, A History* (New York: Random House).

Wilhelm, Richard, and Baynes, Cary F. (translators); *The I Ching* (Princeton, N.J.: Princeton University Press; Bollingen Series XIX, 1967).

Williams, Dr Roger J.; *Nutrition Against Disease* (New York: Pitman Publishing Corp., 1971).

Zax, Melvin, and Stricker, George; *The Study of Abnormal Behaviour* (New York: Macmillan, 1969).

Zorn, Yogi William; *Yoga for the Mind* (New York: Paperback Library, 1970).

INDEX